Simple Relaxation

D0541205

Laura Mitchell, MCSP, dipTP, is well known
in British physiotherapy and obstetric circles,
particularly in the teaching field. She has
publicised her method through her lectures,
tapes and pamphlets for the medical profession
and through her series of broadcasts on BBC
Radio London, BBC *Woman's Hour*, and on
television. She taught living anatomy at the London
School of Occupational Therapy for thirty years.
Her companion book *Simple Movement* was
published in 1980 (for details see the back of
this book), and in 1984 she published *Healthy Living
Over 55*. This is based on her work for the Central
Independent Television series 'Getting On' and is a
comprehensive guide covering the mental, emotional
and physical sides of life in your later years

Simple Relaxation

THE PHYSIOLOGICAL METHOD

FOR EASING TENSION

Laura Mitchell

WITH DRAWINGS BY

MICHAEL BARTLETT

JOHN MURRAY

Contents

*To all the patients, students and colleagues who have
taught me so much in the past, in the hope that this knowledge
may be of use to others in the future*

Acknowledgements

I want to thank Mrs Audrey Cook who gave me peace and comfort in which to write at her home in Cornwall, Mrs Susan Sinclair who transcribed and typed my manuscript, Mr Michael Bartlett for his excellent drawings, and Mr Roger Hudson of John Murray, whose quick understanding and skill have been such a help.

I am also grateful to many colleagues who have read various chapters and freely given me their time and wise advice, but of course all the opinions expressed here are my responsibility as are any mistakes: Dr R Daley FRCP and Mrs A Daley MCSP; Dr M Goldberg and Mrs L Goldberg MCSP; Dr J Mitchell MD FRCP, Associate Professor in the Faculty of Medicine at the University of British Columbia; Dr W Newnham MB Bch BAO DPM, Consultant Psychiatrist, and Mrs J Abbott MCSP, Superintendent Physiotherapist at the Towers Hospital, Leicester; Miss D Gaskell MCSP, Superintendent Physiotherapist at the Brompton Chest Hospital, London; Mrs J Grieve BSc, Tutor in Anatomy and Physiology at the London School of Occupational Therapy; Miss J McKenna MCSP, Senior Obstetric Physiotherapist at the Royal Free Hospital, London.

I am indebted to Professor J S Buchwald, Professor of Physiology at the University of California Los Angeles, for permission to reproduce a simplified version of drawings (p. 23) from her article in the *American Journal of Physical Medicine* vol 46 1967, no 1 pp. 104-113. The photograph of a lung on p. 95 is by kind permission of the President and Council of the Royal College of Surgeons, and of the antenatal patient Mrs Dunning on p. 98 by kind permission of her and Mrs S Harrison, senior obstetric physiotherapist at the United Norwich Hospitals. The four photographs on pp. 29-32 are by permission of London Express News and Feature Service.

Part 1

1   Disease spells Dis-Ease

The purpose of this book is to help people who find themselves tense and tired, and unable to 'relax'. You may have become aware that at work or at home you feel continually tired and edgy, and that you are losing your temper more often—in fact that you are becoming stressed. Busy people of high intelligence and sensitivity are most susceptible to this. The consumption of sedatives, tranquillisers, pain killers, alcohol, tobacco and coffee increases yearly. In 1979 a total of 41.85 million prescriptions for tranquillisers, sedatives and hypnotics was issued in the United Kingdom at a cost of £43.98 million.

Possibly you suffer from persistent chest pains, tummy pains or even ulcers, asthma or skin disorders, and your doctor may have told you to try and relax to help these conditions. Figures for the killer diseases in which stress is a contributing factor, are really frightening. Deaths in England and Wales from coronary heart disease were 805 per million for men and 348 per million for women in 1941. Thirty years later these had shot up to 2,603 and 1,579 respectively.[2]

You may have tried many methods of relaxation without success; you may have wearied of the search and feel it to be pointless. I hope that you may find what you seek here.

The first part of the book explains the fascinating process by which anyone learns to make muscles work. It then shows how this can go wrong and tension build up. I have tried to use ordinary language throughout, e.g. nerve rather than neuron, forebrain for cerebrum, etc. Those interested in physiological details will find them all in the books listed in the references. The book goes on to teach a scientific method of controlling tension, and changing it to enjoyable ease, at will. The method is called Physiological Relaxation because it is based on the rules governing the working of the muscles in the body that are under the control of the will. The method has been widely used for over twenty years. It is now practised in many hospitals in this and forty other countries and by literally thousands of people who find it easy and helpful to use at home and during a busy day—dictating, typing, shopping, driving etc.

You will not be asked to think fanciful thoughts like floating in space. No self hypnosis is involved. You will not be asked to do strange things like 'dwelling on your solar plexus' or 'feeling your warm blood coursing through your arms'. This is not another form of meditation, although I do know that some groups use this method to obtain relaxation before meditating (see Chapter 7). You will not be asked to perform any gymnastic exercises or use visualization or distraction methods. This is not another Yoga book nor another massage book. It does not dictate complicated breathing controls. You may have tried some of these methods without success, and are now rather sceptical of anyone mentioning the word Relax. You may even say 'Rest is not for me, I believe in keeping busy'. But do you realize that rest is one of the in-built rules of the human body?

The heart, which you might imagine works night and day all through your life, actually rests longer than it works. Every time the heart beats there is a rest period of approximately .5 of a second and a work period of approximately .3 of a second for its muscle.[3] The uterus, also, when it is working to deliver the baby inside it, rests longer than it works, adding up the working and resting periods, during the whole labour.[4] So what goes for parts of the body, goes for the whole as well. Everyone needs rest if they are to work efficiently. Above all they need to get rid of unnecessary muscle work which only wastes energy in unused tension. It is noticeable how much care is given to the rest periods of the astronauts in space. One might imagine when their time is so limited, and each second costs so many dollars that they would forego rest and just get on with the work. But no, their training experts insist on their frequent rest periods.

When you read this book you will learn how to change tension to ease, yourself, by following the physiological laws which govern your body. You now take advantage of these laws instead of having them take advantage of you.

The method is completely simple, easy to learn, and can be practised and used in the course of everyday life without disrupting whatever one is engaged in—during meetings, driving a car, during dental treatments, etc. I hope it will particularly suit people who know that they suffer from tension but prefer to work, in private, from a book, since they fear that other people may think they are failing in their job if they admit to any form of stress. Once you have mastered the very easy routine of physiological relaxation that forms the core of this book, there are several ways to use it. As well as using it during your actual working day, as I have suggested, you can use it to have a quick thorough rest or to go to sleep. You will find it useful when in pain or during an anxious period. It is much used in classes for antenatal mothers. They find the technique useful during pregnancy when it prevents undue fatigue, actually during labour, and postnatally, when there seems so much to do and inexperienced mothers tend to suffer from nervous tension and fatigue.

People with breathing difficulties, bronchitis and asthma etc., have found great relief by using this method. It is also increasingly being used in psychiatric clinics. Ballet students find that by obtaining proper relaxation they can perfect their muscular control.

Business men and all who work under pressure—auctioneers, public speakers, actors—find they can use physiological relaxation either fully, to prepare for meetings and important appearances, or in part during them. The exactness of the method appeals to men. Throughout the book I have referred to the reader as 'he' except in the section in Chapter 6, for antenatal mothers. This is simply for convenience, not because women are any less interested than men.

You will also learn from this method how to tell when someone else is feeling tense and this is certainly helpful in dealing with them at interviews, family discussions and the like. Other people too will find you more congenial if you are relaxed rather than in fighting trim. You are, I hope, going to learn a new skill which will make life pleasanter both for you and for those with whom you spend it. You will also, probably, by preventing unnecessary stress, live longer.

As you read this book you may well find that you are asking yourself 'Why should I believe her? What reasons has she for being so definite and so different in her approach to tension?'

To answer these questions I shall have to give you some personal reminiscences. So if you can't be bothered with that, skip the rest of this chapter. Then you will just have to believe what I say later without proof.

Once upon a time—around 1957—I was admitted as an emergency to hospital with collapsed discs in the neck and grievous pain down the arm. I had a long history of arthritis of the spine and was used to a good deal of pain, off and on. So I had taken no notice, a good many pain killing pills, and carried on working. Finally the pain got beyond endurance, and I called for medical help. The doctors admitted me to hospital within the hour. I was put under sedation, and propped up in bed with an adjustable collar to try to fix the neck; as there was so much deformity they couldn't apply plaster of Paris immediately. This was accomplished after several weeks of rest, and I wore the horrid thing for several months.

While I was in hospital I became aware that I had two different pains. One was a pain down my arm, with definite areas of fierceness. This was due to the pressure of the deformed vertebrae on the roots of the spinal nerves and was only relieved by the pain killer I was given four hourly. The other pain was a continuous ache in my neck, body and arms. It seemed to me this might be due to the very odd position I had adopted, and into which I seemed to be fixed. So I tried to relax. First the contrast method in which one tenses all muscles, indiscriminately, and then tries to 'let them go'. I had been teaching this for 20 years—indeed it is still being taught. It made not the slightest difference.

Then I tried various breath controls, as I had studied and taught many of them: so-called abdominal breathing, very popular in the nineteen thirties; deep inward breath followed by long outward breath; concentration on listening to the breathing. All no use.

As I had trained in dancing with the Margaret Morris Movement, I had learned the most popular methods of producing relaxation and indeed had taught them. I tried them all. Concentrating on various parts of the body and telling each in turn to relax beginning at the feet and ending at the head. Moving each joint in turn, tensing muscles in turn and 'relaxing'. Lifting each part in turn and letting it fall heavily on the bed. Visualizing the body getting heavier or like a floppy doll and falling through the bed. None of this helped.

Then I tried Couéism—'every day in every way I am getting better and better' repeated ad lib. I felt worse, and very silly as well, for the pain persisted. It seemed to me by now that rather a heavy elephant was lying across my shoulders.

Then suddenly one day it occurred to me that if I could recognize this odd posture that I was in, and work my way out of it, by doing the opposite movement in each joint, it might give me relief. It worked. The relief was enormous. Gradually I felt relaxation spread over me. I even slept. This in spite of the other pain still being present. I continued doing this morning, noon and night or in fact whenever I felt the old tense positions coming back. I was infinitely more comfortable.

When I went back to work it seemed to me that among the group of patients I treated, those who would certainly also suffer from two pains, were the antenatal mothers. They would have the pain of labour, and also the tenseness due to this. So I started teaching the antenatal mothers the little bit of technique I had developed in hospital for myself. They told me later it helped them greatly in labour.

For years I worked at this method. I studied the positions people adopted in various states of stress and found they were exactly the same as I had discovered in myself. The amazing thing was that whatever the cause of the stress, the resulting positions seemed to be the same. I studied pictures of distressed people of all types and ages. I watched all my tensed patients, like a hawk—women in labour, a child having an asthma attack, a tense businessman—and found again and again the same positions exactly in every joint. It was, of course, more noticeable in some than in others, and varied in degree as the emotional state of the patient varied.

At the same time I was studying the physiology of muscle and muscle work all over again. I was lucky to be teaching living anatomy to the students of the London School of Occupational Therapy. Therefore I had plenty of students to help me clarify my mind and make me keep up to date with current physiological ideas.

I applied the physiological rules by which voluntary muscles change any body position to another position. I then taught patients to change their own positions of tension, one by one, to the exactly opposite positions, and to feel the result in each joint. This had to be very exact work, and based carefully on the physiological laws. I therefore called the method Physiological Relaxation. It seemed to be helpful for the varied types of patients I was treating.

It took several years of trial and error and work with hundreds of patients, antenatal and others, before I finally selected the very simple words you will find in Chapter 4. I then had to prove their efficiency by further use of them, both by other people teaching the method, and by myself. It was only when others reported, that they had found the method successful with patients who had had no tuition from me, that I was really satisfied. I had to have proof that it was the method rather than myself that got results. Some people think that the personality of the teacher is important in getting patients to relax. I believe that this is too circumscribed a view, and in any case takes the responsibility from the patient for the control of his own body. This is not helpful. Each patient should become more and more responsible for the control of his tensions. He should never become dependent on his teacher, or on anyone else.

I had to find words that were appropriate but entirely non medical; for example when talking about 'the shoulder girdle' (clavicle and scapula) I had just to use the term 'shoulders' because any lay person knows that area. He would find the 'girdle' muddling, even though, in fact, it is anatomically correct. I had to find simple words that could be easily memorised, and that would always produce the exact desired joint and muscle changes. They had to be acceptable to all kinds of people from the young antenatal mother to the older businessman or nervous child. They had to be unambiguous and exact: the result of saying 'Drag your jaw down' is quite different from 'Drop your jaw'. The words had also to fit any patient in any position, so that 'forwards' 'backwards' etc. could not be used.

This was quite a task, and of course took years, but I found it all fascinating. The method was gradually being used for the benefit of men, women and children, and it was thrilling to find it helped so many people. In 1963 I was asked to take part in the section on 'Stress' at the World Confederation of Physical Medicine in Copenhagen. Since then I have published several pamphlets, two cassettes (one for antenatal mothers and one for stress patients) and have been asked to lecture about the method all over Britain and in Ireland, Italy and Canada. I have done a series about it on BBC Radio London. The result is that Physiological Relaxation is now widely used in hospitals, clinics, and by individuals.

I have personally continued to use it and without such a technique in my daily life I should have found it difficult to carry on all I have undertaken. I had the misfortune to develop a bone infection, which lasted some years, in spite of the most skilful and devoted care of my doctors and surgeon. This involved a good deal of pain, not least when the hip joint came out of position when I was alone for 12 hours. The ability to undo my muscular tensions induced by pain helped enormously.

In Chapters 2 and 3 we will discuss how your muscles work and how you control them so that you can tune into the control system for your own benefit.

2   Nerves, Muscles and Fear

I am fearfully and wonderfully made Psalm 139 v. 14

Of course muscular tension is an excellent thing. Without it we would not be able to move a finger. It gets things done. You need it to eat your breakfast. If you are crossing a field full of cows and you suddenly realize that one of them has a ring in his nose and is hurtling in your direction, you will certainly need tension to reach that fence and scramble over it. Muscular tension is only dangerous when it is not used for work, is repeated, and then leads to stress.

Let us consider how muscular tension or action is produced. There are two ways in which the muscles attached to our bones perform work. The first is called voluntary movement (planned action) as in eating breakfast, and the second reflex movement (unplanned action), as in running from the bull. These actions are controlled by nerves carrying messages to and from the brain and to and from the spinal cord. The brain and spinal cord together are called the central nervous system, in which we are told there are about 12 billion nerves.

There are three kinds of these nerves:

1.   Those that carry messages from the central nervous system: motor nerves.

2.   Those that carry messages to the central nervous system: sensory nerves.

Outside the spinal cord these two are found in one 'mixed nerve' in which there are thousands of nerve fibres conveying different kinds of messages.[1]

3.   Those that relay messages from one part of the central nervous system to another: multipolar nerves.

The brain has special areas which control specialized functions, e.g. voluntary muscular activity (motor area, see drawing p. 20) or receive specialized information, e.g. of joint position (sensory area, see drawing p. 20), control of balance and muscle co-ordination (cerebellum).

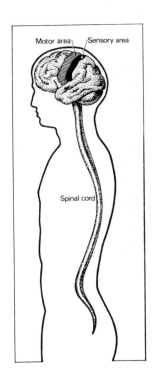

1 The central nervous system

MOTOR NERVE ENDINGS

All nerve fibres have specialized endings which can only perform one function. Motor nerve fibres end in muscle as motor end plates (see drawing p. 21).

They are, if you like, the 'out' lines from the central nervous system. Each motor end plate controls a varying number of muscle fibres and makes them work.[2] In the tiny thumb muscles there are numerous nerve fibres to control the muscles, which is why we can do very clever movements with our thumbs. There are fewer nerve endings per muscle in our larger coarser muscles like those in the buttock, which really don't do very exacting movements, just raise and lower us and some other large movements, like lifting a leg backwards.[3]

SENSORY NERVE ENDINGS

The sensory nerves, the 'in' lines to the central nervous system, have specialized nerve endings.[4] They are selective in what feeling or taste they convey. For example, those in the mouth register various tastes and consistencies: acid, sweet, hard, soft, etc. Those in the skin of the finger tips can distinguish very exact textures like velvet or linen; those in and around the joints distinguish their precise positions (see drawing p. 22).

We can only get a sensation with its selective information from a nerve ending especially constructed to receive that feeling. The feeling will be conveyed by messages along relays of nerves, eventually ending in an area of the brain that registers that special sensation. Those nerve endings which convey sensations from the skin will only do that, those that convey joint sensation will only do that and *nothing else*.[5]

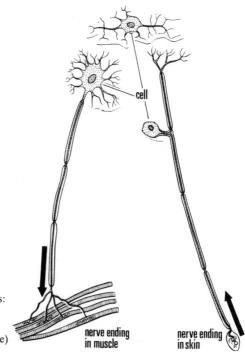

2 Nerves carrying messages:
a motor nerve (left),
sensory nerve (right),
and multipolar nerve (above)

cell

nerve ending
in muscle

nerve ending
in skin

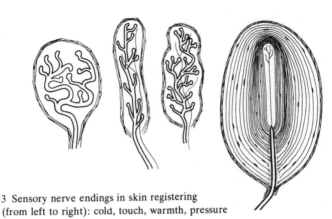

3 Sensory nerve endings in skin registering
(from left to right): cold, touch, warmth, pressure

The object of this description of our nerves is to explain why, when you begin to perform this method of relaxation, you will be asked to register the exact position of your joints and sensations of skin pressure. This is because you have the appropriate sensory nerve endings there, whose job it is to do exactly that.[6] You can register the *result* of muscle work indirectly in this way through the feel of other parts that do have the necessary nerve endings, e.g. skin, joints. You will please *not* try to register the state of the muscle tension because you have no nerve endings in the muscle that can convey this information to your consciousness.[7] Certainly there are sensory nerve endings inside muscle that do convey the sensation of stretch (Spindles). There are also sensory nerve endings (Golgi) around the tendons of muscles. But their sensations travel to the spinal cord, mid and hind brain, *not* to the conscious part of the brain.[8] Therefore it is as useless to ask a person consciously to feel tension in his muscle, as it would be to ask him to taste an orange by putting his big toe into it. He does not possess the necessary apparatus. Just try this little experiment. Shut your eyes, leave your left arm wherever it happens to be. Don't move it. Try to feel the position of your elbow and wrist, whether they are straight or bent and how much. I'm sure you can do that without any difficulty. Open your eyes and look. You will surely find you were right for each joint. Now shut your eyes again and see if you can feel the state of the muscles above and below the elbow joint, back and front. I don't think you will be able to do so. Don't worry, there's nothing wrong with you. Nobody can do that, although unfortunately many people are often asked to do so when trying to learn how to relax.

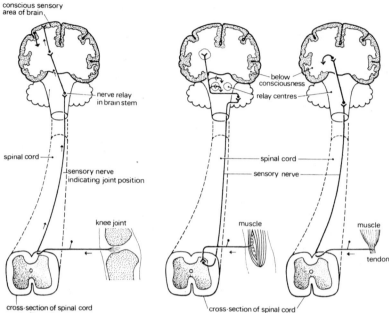

4 **Destination of sensory nerves**

Left—Joint sends message indicating its position up to consciousness where it can be registered. Appropriate messages can then be sent down from the cortex at will

Centre—Muscle sends message indicating stretching to several parts of brain, all of which are below the conscious level. Appropriate messages are immediately relayed back down spinal cord and then along motor nerves to muscles without any conscious control

Right—Tendon sends message indicating the amount of pull on it to brain below consciousness. Appropriate messages are immediately relayed back down spinal cord

You have no nerve endings there to convey information to your conscious brain of the state of muscle tension, so it is not surprising that such people are disappointed.[9]

Now let us see how this central nervous system plus the nerves control our movements.

VOLUNTARY MOVEMENT

This means movements under the control of our will.[10] We tell our bodies to do something, for example eat our breakfast.

We then cut up, lift the fork, open the mouth, chew, swallow and so do the job. The initiation of the action is our own will, and the nerve paths used begin in the motor area of the fore brain. The messages pass down the nerves in the spinal cord and then out to the chosen muscles along motor nerves.[11] (drawing p. 23)

REFLEX MOVEMENT

We do not plan this as we do in voluntary movement.[12] It has developed as a body or life-saving mechanism, e.g. withdrawing the hand from a hot surface,[13] blinking when an object comes towards the eye. We feel the pain after the hand has been withdrawn. The eye sees the object but before this information can reach the thinking brain, messages have passed between appropriate nerves and made the eyelid close quickly. The initiation here therefore is something outside the body—the object attacking the eye. The path is a sensory nerve into the central nervous system with a message of the danger, just as you would ring up a telephone exchange. The multipolar nerves relay the message to the appropriate motor nerves, just as the telephone exchange operator would connect you with the line you wanted. These messages pass out of the central nervous system by motor nerves and cause appropriate action, in this case making the muscle of the eyelid close it.

The Stretch Reflex If a muscle is suddenly stretched, this is registered in the muscle spindle, the only nerve ending leading from muscle which records sensation; this only records 'stretch'.[14] This sensation does not reach the fore brain, instead its messages pass direct to motor nerves in the spinal cord, which cause the same muscle to shorten immediately.[15] A good example of this is the knee jerk we all know. When the doctor taps the tendon just below the knee, this stretches the muscle which lies above the knee and which is attached to this tendon. This muscle immediately contracts and the lower leg kicks forward.

This reflex is most used by the body to preserve our upright posture. If we were falling forwards the back muscles would be stretched. By reflex, they therefore contract, before we are aware of it, and so pull us upright again.[16]

5 The stretch reflex at
the knee: cause and effect

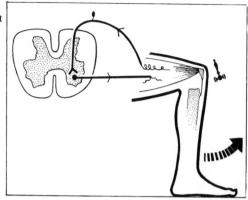

The Fear Reflex   There are complicated reflexes like
the fear reflex which dominate many muscles and some glands. This
gets the body ready to fight or run in the face of a threat. There are
some people who react by inertia instead—almost like paralysis. We
are not dealing with these but with the more usual result of 'fight or
flight'. The fear reflex depends for its stimulation on happenings
both outside and inside the body. The sight of an opponent, the
sound of a bomb, the emotion of fear, pain, jealousy, etc., the
memory of past unhappiness, initiate the reflex and immediately
without control of the will, messages flash along nerves to the
cerebellum and mid brain, suitable association takes place by the
multipolar nerves and orders pass out through the motor nerves
from the spinal cord for the action of fighting or running.[17]

From the list above of external stimulants which bring on the fear
reflex, you have probably guessed that it is this reflex which is the
immediate cause within the body of tension and stress. We cannot
escape these stimulants; they are the pressures of life as most of us
live it today. Even if we try to live an easy life, we would still
confront some of them. Equally the fear reflex is an essential part of
our survival kit. What we can do is use the paths and laws of
voluntary movement to get ourselves out of the tensed positions
produced by the fear reflex, and so stop its control over us,
whenever we wish to do so.

If the brain receives messages of a negative emotion—fear, com-
petition, dislike, apprehension and so on—immediately and without conscious direction, the primitive fear reflex goes into action
and activates the fighting muscles.

This primitive animal reflex developed when fighting or running were the only possible answers to danger. You attacked the smaller enemy and you ran away from the bigger one. An amazing sequence of physiological changes take place in the body to further this activity.

The heart speeds up, the blood pressure rises, the breath is either hurried or held deep inside, adrenaline is produced from the adrenal glands and poured into the blood stream, so that extra sugar is released for the muscles to use. Blood is sent to the working muscles and drained from other areas. Digestion of food is interrupted and the capacity to think may be diminished. Clotting of the blood is enhanced, in case of injury.

This is all very useful if, in fact, we are fighting or running, i.e. discharging our stress. But more often in a modern situation the muscles don't actually make us fight or run, because we are in a situation in which neither action will help us. Yet our fighting muscles bounce into activity immediately we receive the messages of danger. Indeed, the memory of frustration, pain, anger, jealousy, etc. will also do this and the muscles, once triggered, stay fixed and unproductive, tense but undischarged.

Here is what happens.

STRESS POSITIONS

The Head   The head comes forward. If the stress is due to grief or pain, the head may bend right down with the chin in. If the stress is caused by anger or apprehension, the chin juts out and the whole head moves forwards on the neck.

The Arms   The shoulders are lifted upwards towards the ears and held there. The upper arms hug the chest either at the sides, or in front, while the elbows bend up.

The Hands   The fingers and thumbs curl up to form a punch and the hands may indeed clench each other. The person may clasp some object tightly, or a man often puts his hands in his trouser pockets and keeps turning his money over.

The Legs if sitting down   A woman tends to sit sideways on the edge of the chair and wind one leg around the other. Both men and women usually cross their legs and then the top foot is held rigidly upwards, or moves rapidly up and down at the ankle. The accent is on the up movement (dorsiflexion).

The Legs if standing   The person may cross and uncross his legs continuously. We often see this performance by a platform speaker. Equally he may walk about in an aimless manner. 'I can't keep still.'

The Body   The body bends forwards and is usually held fairly rigid. This may cause pain in the back.

The Breathing   The breath is either held on an inward gasp, or it is quickened so that the upper chest moves rapidly up and down. The accent is always on the inward breath.

The Face   The jaw is clamped tightly shut, and the teeth often grind together. The lips are tightly closed. The tongue cleaves to the roof of the mouth. The brows corrugate and the eyes may either screw up as in grief or pain or open wide as in real or imagined danger.

Maybe you recognize one or more of the positions as a habit of yours. Maybe you remember falling into the whole pattern at some time of deep emotion, pain, danger, or apprehension. Have you ever noticed other people in these positions? Perhaps on the television or in pictures in newspapers? Perhaps you remember some meeting or family discussion where another member, noticeably clenched a fist, or pointed a rigid forefinger at you, thrusting out his chin in your direction and speaking in a hard angry voice. Or perhaps he sat silent, in a hunched position, narrowing his eyes and grinding his teeth.

I am not exaggerating. People do that. Only last year, when I thought I had already developed control of my own tensions, I discovered I held my breath when I was transplanting tiny seedlings. This was obviously ridiculous. I couldn't imagine why I always got so breathless and exhausted, there on my knees when I was only planting out—a job I loved doing—which requires the minimum of effort.

Then I realized I was in the grip of the same old fear reflex, because I was so anxious not to damage my precious plants. To correct this I therefore made myself breathe consciously with my diaphragm occasionally while planting, and I was never breathless again doing this easy pleasant work. You will quickly learn this gentle diaphragmatic control (Chapter 4 p. 52).

It is interesting that the same pattern of movement is always adopted by men, women and children. The degree of tension of course varies on different occasions, and from one person to another, and may include any or all of these positions. This strangely inappropriate behaviour can build up and up until it produces real physical changes and pain—headaches, neck and backache, stomach disorders including ulcers, persistent tiredness, changes in the walls of blood vessels, etc. It can actually kill. Remember the heart pounding away at an increased rate, with no respite, plus the heightened blood pressure, and increased clotting facilities of the blood.

Cardiologists tell us that maintaining a tight hand grip leads to increased heart work with a rise in blood pressure and pulse rate. In those who already suffer from heart disease, angina may be provoked. If as frequently occurs the breath is held at the same time, the pressure of blood in the veins rises, less blood is pumped out of the heart and temporary unconsciousness may result. Carrying packs on the back using larger muscle groups has no such effect, nor do intermittent arm movements, if the grip is intermittent.

Look at the pictures of people in stress positions on pp. 29-31 and you will see examples of what happens. Then compare the unstressed happy person on p. 32 and notice the exact opposite pattern. This is what you are going to be able to achieve at will.

The fear reflex, being initially a life-saving one, is going to be part of us all our lives. Sometimes we need it, but we also need to learn to dispose of it when it is not needed and instead of being a life-saver, it has become a killer.

We now know that the body itself tries to deal with the fear situation by manufacturing its own tranquillizer in the brain, called endomorphine. So we are on the right lines when we try to control the fear reflex, instead of allowing it to ravage us uncontrolled.

Detective Sergeant Edmund Murray, Sir Winston Churchill's bodyguard, at the door of Sir Winston's home as he lay dying in 1965.

Mrs Dennis Healey being interviewed in 1974.

Notice the similar tense positions of these three different people in different worrying circumstances. Their heads are pushed forward and their necks appear to have practically vanished. The spines are curved forward; arms are close to the body, with all elbows bent up except one. Hands are clenched and all legs are crossed.

Miss Vickie Lewis, a 1967 debutante, waiting to take part in a dress show.

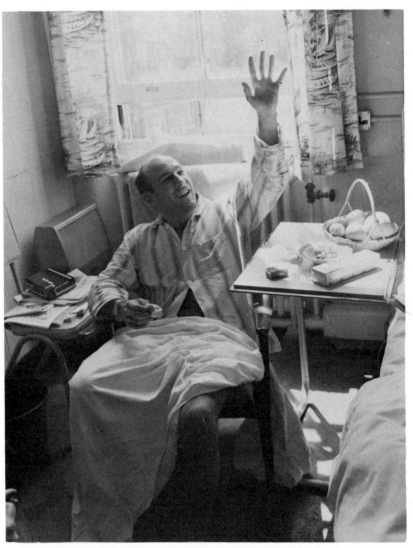

Stirling Moss in hospital in 1962 recovering from a motor racing accident.

Compare this relaxed picture with the other three. His head is up, his eyes are open and his mouth is loose. He does not bend forward. His arms are away from his body and his fingers and thumb are stretched. His legs are not crossed.

3   How Your Body Moves

The beauty and logic intrinsic in the design of the nervous system
A. C. Guyton

When cataloguing (p. 26) the various tense positions which different parts of our bodies adopt at the prompting of the fear reflex, I said at the end that they amounted to a *pattern* of movement. Now it is not only reflex movement which falls into patterns. All the voluntary movements that we make are parts of patterns,[1] the difference being that the conscious brain plays a part in the establishment of these latter ones and they are therefore subject to our will. The technique of physiological relaxation which I hope you will acquire through this book is itself a pattern of movement, therefore it is important to say more about how we learn patterns throughout our lives. The more we understand about a learning process, the better we learn.

PATTERNS OF MOVEMENT

While the fore brain gives the order for specific work, it does not order exact muscular activity.[2] The order would never be 'use your arm muscles'. It would be 'pick up the box' or 'lay down the pen' etc. The muscle work is selected in the central nervous system. The brain acts like a computer. Information, being received from outside and within the body by messages from the sensory nerves, decides the output of muscular activity needed to achieve the desired result. All the time the performance is taking place it is registered, corrected and imprinted in the sensory area of the brain by these millions of messages. When the final result has been registered there the muscles are told to stop working and this result is also imprinted. Thus the pattern of movement is established.

At birth there are about ten thousand million cells in the brain.[3] These cells develop their function as—and only as—they are used. This is one reason why the early years are so important.

When a baby is learning how to grasp and examine objects he reaches towards something he has seen and wants. He is using his will to initiate a voluntary movement. As he touches the teddy bear his sensitive finger tips flash the information up to his brain that he has reached it and is touching it. He then curls his fingers and thumbs around it, and decides to put it into his mouth to appreciate its feel a bit more with his sensitive lips.

As he bends his shoulder and elbow, and yet still grasps the teddy bear with his hand and directs it towards his mouth, he is learning a very complicated pattern which is being registered all the time in the sensory part of his fore brain. If this is satisfactory, in that the resulting feeling pleases him and agrees with what he wanted to do at the beginning of the performance, i.e. pick up the teddy and 'explore' it, he is delighted. He then repeats the action with other objects and so builds up what is known as a 'pattern of movement', in this case the pattern for picking something up and tasting it. So don't stop his attempts. His central nervous system is busy learning to translate work orders into muscle work to suit, and is practising receiving information about this.[4]

It is because of the personal training you gave yourself for months on end with enjoyable results that today you are able to handle and drink from a tankard of beer, or a mug of coffee or a cup and saucer of tea and to differentiate, both in taste and manner of drinking.

Don't think each skill is easy to learn.[5] A child works very hard every day, all day long, with only time off to eat and sleep and smile a bit, to train a few patterns of movement.[6] But it gets easier with practice.

After twelve months of continuous activity,[7] of practice and repetition, he can probably stand up, maybe walk and perform a few skills with his hands. He might perhaps be able to eat an egg with a spoon by putting it exactly into his mouth, because he has enjoyed the taste, instead of his ear, or all over his face which he did when he was learning. But he couldn't do anything so complicated as buttoning, tying a bow, or running. These he will gradually add to his repertoire of patterns of movement. He can go on adding to these skills and filing them in the sensory area of his brain all his life—bicycling, typing, dancing, etc. You are going to add one more, I hope, by learning physiological relaxation by voluntary control in Chapter 4. This will be fairly easy for you as a result of the childhood and later training you have already given yourself. We will be using exactly the same method.

Why did the baby use his fingers to pick up the teddy? Why did he put it in his mouth? Because babies are wise. Look at this diagram

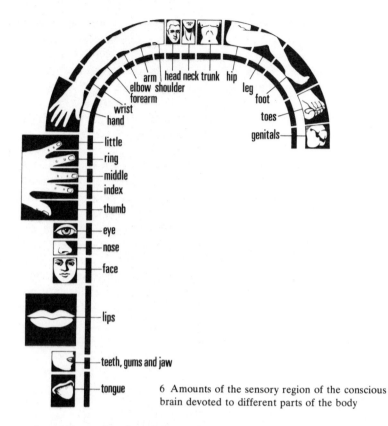

arm | head neck trunk | hip
elbow shoulder
forearm
wrist
hand

leg
foot
toes
genitals

little
ring
middle
index
thumb
eye
nose
face
lips
teeth, gums and jaw
tongue

6 Amounts of the sensory region of the conscious brain devoted to different parts of the body

and wonder at the size of the areas in the brain that receive sensory feelings. You will see that the fingers and especially the thumb, also the lips, have proportionately the largest areas to register sensation in the whole body. That is why babies use their hands and mouths for learning movements.[8] You are going to use these facts when you train yourself in physiological relaxation for relief of stress.

This intimate association of muscle work and feeling is repeated again and again and used to develop every single muscular skill we possess. These are all laid down and labelled in the *sensory* area of the fore brain as 'Patterns of Movement'.[9]

Next time you are driven crazy by your first-born dropping his belongings one by one over the side of his pram don't say 'naughty, naughty'. Thank God he is training his pattern of movement. He has learned grasping by his grasping (flexor) muscles. Now he practises the reverse using the opposite muscles (extensors) of his hands and fingers. These two groups perform exactly opposite movements. This system of opposite groups of muscles is found all over the body, e.g. those that close the hand and those that open it, those that bend the head forwards and those that extend it backwards. Of course the baby is also learning more subtle differences in muscle control, in this case the difference between dropping and laying down. So he is practising over and over again until he learns by doing.

Thus we gradually acquire very exact orders in our vocabulary of movement.[10] These trigger off the necessary pathways of nerve control to selected muscle groups to carry out the required movement. This work is monitored all the time it is happening in the sensory (registering feeling) part of the brain. This registers sensation continuously so that the desired result can be achieved. Conscious feeling from voluntary movement is registered by skin and joints, *not* from inside the muscles because there are no nerve endings there registering tension which reach consciousness. The sensory information from muscles and tendons is registered in the spinal cord and hind and mid brain and of course is helpful in building up the complete picture of the activity. But it is absolutely necessary in training yourself in any skill to know what feelings can be recognised and what cannot (See drawing on p. 23).

STRESS AND THE FEAR REFLEX

Have you ever watched a young child trying to fondle a cat? It consists of a series of pinches, bangs, probably some hard rubbing interspersed with an odd prod with the forefinger. Why can't he do it gently? Because he is still in the process of mastering his very complicated muscle control of arm, hand, and fingers in response to sensation received. Some people never achieve control of their own muscles. Do you remember the classic response of the parlour maid in *Punch* after breaking something? 'It came to bits in me hand, Mum.' Really what she was saying was 'I wasn't paying attention to the sensations reaching my brain of the shape, texture, and movement of the jug in my hands. Having received this information I did not send the appropriate messages, through my central nervous system to handle the jug suitably while drying it. I therefore used incorrect muscle work and this destroyed the jug.'

That may sound silly or pedantic but it's exactly what you and I do, when we allow our bodies to become controlled by the fear reflex, which produces muscle work suitable for fighting or running, when we are, in fact, just sitting in our office, talking to someone. And the result is something much more serious that a broken jug and it is called stress. It may be a dead you if you persist in it.

THE VICIOUS CIRCLE

Tense positions of the body create more tension by sending to the spinal cord and to many parts of the brain continuous information that the body is prepared for fight or flight and therefore is in danger. Because of this, messages continually flash out to all fighting muscles to accentuate their tension. Stress can thus be built up and become a self perpetuating vicious circle.[11] It is this continuing stress that can do so much harm. The physiological relaxation technique cuts through the vicious circle by sending feelings of ease, at will, from every joint and from the highly sensitive skin to the brain instead of the messages of positions of tension which perpetuate the fear reflex. We will therefore enhance the feelings of ease streaming up to the brain by noticing carefully the results of the changed positions. Thus we get the brain to 'monitor' them, to store and 'label' them. Ease and fear do not live side by side. The fear reflex subsides.[12]

WHY MUSCLES GET TIRED

What is the difference chemically inside the stressed working muscles and relaxed ones? Does it matter? It certainly does to the owner of the muscles. Muscles can work in several ways.[13] There is a wide terminology describing these ways so I will try to link terms up.[14]

Muscles are composed of bundles of fibres. These fibres work fully or not at all. (The All or None Law).[15] Therefore a suitable number of fibres go on duty for any particular task—many to lift a piano, few to lift a feather, none at all if not given work to do.[16]

Isotonic means the muscle works, retains the same amount of 'tone' i.e. power or number of muscle fibres in action, and is either shortening or being lengthened.

Concentric means it is working and shortening e.g. the biceps shortens to bend up your elbow.

Eccentric means it is working and being lengthened in the process, e.g. the biceps works and is lengthened by the pull of gravity as it lowers the weight of the forearm slowly downwards. If the forearm is allowed to fall by the force of gravity there is no controlling muscle work.

Isometric and static both mean the same thing—that the muscle is working and not changing length e.g. the elbow once bent is held stationary by the working biceps.

In each case muscles use up oxygen and glycogen (sugar) and give off carbon dioxide and lactic acid as waste products. If the blood supply through the muscle is flowing well, it brings fresh supplies of glucose (sugar) and oxygen continuously and the waste products are easily carried away in the fluid in which all the cells of the body are bathed (tissue fluid). The waste products are eventually collected by the blood and taken to the lungs, kidneys and skin and excreted.

Now when muscles change their length while working they have a benign pumping action on the blood stream. This keeps the flow on the move. This does not happen when the muscles work to hold a joint stationary because the increased muscle bulk which bunches up, presses on the smaller vessels with no respite and impedes the blood and lymph flow.

This work without movement (isometric i.e. static) is the hardest way muscles can work. If it is continued over a long period the muscles become depleted of oxygen and glycogen and sodden with their own waste products, lactic acid, etc. Eventually the area becomes stiff and sore and the muscles are unable to work properly.

Try this experiment and prove it for yourself. Raise your arm from your side above your head and then lower it slowly. Do it now, and I think you will find you could continue quite happily for a long time. The muscles that raised and lowered your arm were changing length as they did so (working concentrically and eccentrically).

Now put your arm high above your head and keep it there—stationary. The muscles that lifted it up before are now working strongly all the time to hold it up and they are not changing length. They are working statically (isometrically). You will soon feel tired and uncomfortable and want to lower the weight of your arm.

This is the way (statically) in which muscles work under the influence of the fear reflex. So no wonder stressed people become tired and irritable. No wonder they need to learn how these miserable muscles can be relaxed and given a rest and a life-saving fresh supply of blood. Blood flows easily through and around relaxed muscles and so refreshes the whole area.

The importance of this whole subject of muscle chemistry for our investigation of tension is born out by a piece of research described by Dr Herbert Benson in his book *Relaxation Response* (see Chapter 7 page 113). It has been discovered that an injection of lactate can produce anxiety.[17] We have already seen that lactic acid is one of the waste products which abound in static activity.

RECIPROCAL RELAXATION

Assuming mine is a body under stress, what orders will I choose to give it to change the pattern of stress to a pattern of ease and so break that vicious circle that is exhausting the muscles and get the blood flowing freely through them again? Certainly not 'relax'. 'Relax' conveys no definite information to produce muscle and position change. It is vague, generalized and ambiguous. We need vivid, exact orders because that is what your body is used to receiving and acting upon. Also we do not have to induce relaxation in all muscles because not all muscles are working. We have only to induce it in the sets of muscles which are working to hold the body ready to fight or run. Fortunately there is a very easy way of doing this by applying another physiological law. This is a remarkable phenomenon which always happens during any muscular activity.

Muscles can work singly but usually they work in groups. When any group works the opposite group *relaxes*. This is called 'Reciprocal Inhibition' or 'Reciprocal Relaxation'.[18] It is a law and it always happens. Surely this is just what we have been looking for—relaxation which is absolutely dependable, which is turned on for us unfailingly, if we carefully select work for the correct opposite group of muscles. We will harness this law.

All we have to do to get relaxation in the tense muscles then is to give orders that will involve their opposite group in exact work. The original tense muscles *must* therefore stop working, i.e. relax. They will have been ordered to do so by the nerves of the central nervous system.

For example, if your shoulders are being held up towards your ears they are in the tense position. We will select the positive order 'Pull your shoulders towards your feet'. As this voluntary action is done by the muscles that pull the shoulders downwards, relaxation is automatically produced in the muscles that held the shoulders up. Notice you must not say 'Relax your shoulders' which does not communicate any specific information. Nor must you say 'Drop your shoulders'. In dropping—if it should happen fully—we would produce a stretching movement by the weight of the shoulders (collar bone and shoulder blade plus the weight of the arm). This would initiate the stretch reflex (p. 24). The upper muscles would be stretched, therefore they would immediately tend to contract again reflexly and the shoulders fly up again back to where they were—on guard. You know what happens when you hit a ball on the end of a bit of elastic anchored on the ground. It comes back at you almost faster than it went. Therefore to avoid this, we say 'Pull your shoulders towards your feet', a positive order which will be transmitted from the fore brain. This automatically overrides the stretch reflex and initiates the 'preprogrammed reciprocal relaxation'[19] that we want. We then say 'stop pulling' and the working muscles relax. You have now produced relaxation in all the muscles of that area. During the action you can easily feel what is happening in your joints, and when, finally, you register the new position of your shoulders, you will be feeling the 'ease position'. You really are using the marvellous mechanism you possess for your own benefit.

Now let us consider the unhappy clenching hands as another example. They were put into that position by the fear reflex because, presumably, it turns them into the most effective blunt instrument available to unarmed man. If we say 'Relax your hands' you simply do not know what to do. We have given you no precise help.

In any case people usually don't even know they are clenching their hands—being part of a reflex it is an automatic response. They may half uncurl the punch, but the position of the fingers and thumbs hardly alter, and the joints and skin continue to send messages to the fore brain while the tendons and muscles are sending messages to the mid and hind brain that they are in a punching position. This perpetuates the vicious circle of stress.

If, however, the order given is 'Stretch your fingers and thumbs out as long as possible' the muscles that stretch your fingers and thumbs work, and the muscles that curl up the hands, and that were holding them in the punch position *must* relax because of the reciprocal relaxation law. These two opposing groups are the extensors and flexors of the fingers and thumbs. They are found in the forearm, extensors at the back and flexors at the front, and some of each in the hand itself.

We ensure that the fingers and thumbs are above a support, for example the chair arms. We then say 'Stop stretching' and we have relaxation in the muscles we ordered to work. The fingers and thumbs lie on the support and there is now relaxation in all muscles controlling the hand. Relaxation is the result of carefully selected orders—an end product. 'Relax' can never itself be an order.

Now we apply the principle contained in that diagram on page 35 showing the amounts of the sensory region of the conscious brain devoted to different parts of the body. If you look again you will see the enormous sensory area that the fingers and especially the thumbs have in the conscious brain. We therefore spend some time registering the joint positions and skin contact, and the final position of the thumbs lying motionless and heavy. We register the finger tips resting on the support, the separated fingers and so on. We are using as fully as possible the mechanism we have developed and used continuously since childhood. In this way we educate the brain to recognize the positions of ease just as it has been registering sensation throughout life when learning various other skills, from sewing to turning on a lathe.

I have talked above about the orders necessary to get reciprocal relaxation in two parts of the body—the shoulders and the hands. The same idea is applied overall and we choose the order for change in every joint of the body, that will cause reciprocal relaxation in the tensed up muscles. If, having obeyed the order, we say 'Stop' to the working muscles, we then have obtained relaxation in both sets of muscles in that area. Eventually as we proceed with this method around the body all muscles will be completely relaxed. The next chapter goes systematically around the body telling you what those orders are and how to carry them out.

We are working with most marvellously designed machinery. We have to select very carefully and very humbly how we use it, and fit in with its dependable laws. These will then give us great benefits.

4 The Technique of Physiological Relaxation

Life — that in me has rest Emily Brontë

Now at last we come to the whole point of this book: to learn the method of Physiological Relaxation. We know that people suffering from undischarged stress adopt an exact pattern of positioning in all their joints (pp. 26-27) and that this may become a vicious circle if not interrupted. We have discussed the facts and laws of muscle control in the body (Chapters 2 and 3). I hope you have therefore developed a very healthy respect for this mechanism. You will then want to fit in with your body's rules which will help you to manipulate it so as to induce relaxation at your own will, fully or in part, at any time of your choice.

The most important facts to remember are:

1. The brain must give a definite order that it recognizes will produce work.[1]

2. The order that I have chosen for you to give to each joint will produce relaxation in the tense group of muscles if you perform the movement exactly indicated by the words.[2] When I say 'Pull your shoulders towards your feet' I mean *pull* not *drop*. Only voluntary activity will produce the reciprocal relaxation in the group opposite to the working group.

3. When I say 'Stop' I mean just that.[3] You stop moving the part and you don't move it again. Don't try to substitute 'relax' for 'stop'. It won't help. You understand 'stop moving': do just that.

4. You register the feeling of the new position as accurately as you possibly can.[4] This requires concentration, if you are not accustomed to it, but is otherwise extremely easy. I will try and assist you in this by describing the shape of your joint, the feelings you should get from your skin, e.g. in your finger tips etc.

5. Remember you will be training yourself in *joint* and *skin* consciousness not muscle consciousness because that is the way the body works. There are no nerves recognising muscle tension reaching your upper brain, therefore you will not waste time and effort

trying to feel it. You will be concentrating on the millions of sensory messages your conscious brain is constantly receiving from your joints and skin as your chosen muscles change their positions.

6. I shall not be trying to mesmerize you or persuade you. I shall only be helping you to train your own conscious brain in discriminating sensations that have always been received there but which you may not have recognized till now.

WORK WITH PARTNER

If you ask someone else to read out the orders to you, he must use a perfectly ordinary voice, not try to lull or influence you in any way. Please choose a partner who considers it to be as important as you do, who has read the book and understands its reasoning and how you are trying to apply it. You might later change places, and read out the instructions for your partner. You will learn a great deal by watching and appreciating the performer's appearance and the timing involved.

Whoever is reading out must not add any bits of his own and must follow the timing of the performer—not attempt to lead him in any way. The important person is the performer, remember, the other is only a voice. He should sit as far away from the performer as is practical, and not interfere in any way with what the performer is doing. The performer is learning to recognize the feelings from his own joints and skin. Let him do so in his own time. As soon as the orders have been memorized, dispense with the reader.

WORKING ALONE

Or you may prefer to work alone and to memorize, at the beginning, the order for each part and then do it on your own. This is perfectly possible. The sequence is

1. arms
2. legs
3. breathing
4. body
5. head
6. face

Or you may put breathing after the body and head changes if you prefer.

The orders in each joint are
1. move and feel
2. stop
3. feel

The words are so simple that very soon you will have memorized them and will be able to perform entirely on your own account. This of course is the whole point of learning. You will be able to control your own body—to be in charge of it and not dominated by it or by anyone else.

Don't try to memorize the exact positions. These will vary slightly each time you use the technique, because you will be starting from a slightly different posture on each occasion. Memorize the *orders*. These *never change*. Keep to the sequence round the body that I have indicated, until you become really proficient. Later on you may change this sequence or only use a part of the technique if you wish. But until you really have this skill well under control, stick to the sequence I have suggested. It has a long record of success.

THE ROOM

Have the room comfortably warm, because you will lose heat as your muscles relax. Otherwise make no special preparations. It is better not to insist on absolute quietness, as this is too artificial and quite unnecessary. When I was developing the method with antenatal mothers we were using a corner room, round which large London buses passed regularly. This didn't worry the mothers at all. You are going to concentrate on what you are doing—not be lulled into lethargy. If you need absolute silence in which to relax the technique wouldn't be much use to you in normal life.

STARTING POSITIONS

There are three positions from which you can choose—one lying and two sitting.

Position A If this position is comfortable it is probably the best to use at first. Lie on the floor on a carpet or rug—not on a bed. Have only one pillow under the head and *no others*. The legs are uncrossed if possible and the hands rest either on tummy or thighs depending on the length of the arms. I prefer you not to have pillows under thighs, etc. because when you begin to relax you will

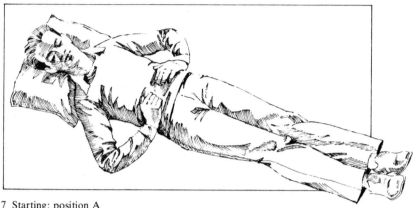

7 Starting: position A

8 Starting: position B

probably find them unnecessary. You don't want to depend on
pillows for comfort. It only confuses the issue. But decide yourself.
If your back feels strained then use a pillow under your thighs at
first.

Position B   Sit on a chair at a table. Sit well back so that
the feet rest on the ground. Then use as many cushions on the table
as you want to raise the height to receive your arms and head. Your
head may lie on one side if you wish.

Position C   The back of the chair must be high enough
to rest the head against. Sit well back in the chair, so that your back

9 Starting: position C

is supported and both feet rest on the floor. The forearms rest on the arms of the chair, as do the hands, which must not hang over the edge. The chair arms must be long enough and broad enough to support the length of all the fingers when stretched out.

I hope you will experiment with all three positions and use them at various times as you prefer. When you have really mastered the technique you can use it in any position whatsoever. The orders, you will find, will always fit. Do *not* change them.

ORDERS TO THE ARMS

Shoulders The order is 'Pull your shoulders towards your feet'. Go on gently pulling them straight down away from your ears and feel what is happening. Do not move anywhere else. Do not pull the shoulders forwards or backwards. When you cannot pull them down any further *stop*. Don't be surprised if they should bounce up again slightly. Often tense people have developed shortened upper muscles due to continually holding the shoulders upwards. In time these will be stretched and the shoulders will stay down. Don't try to hold them down. *Stop pulling.*

Now register the new position of ease. You will probably be able to register that the tops of your shoulders are lower down than they were, i.e. further away from your ears. You may therefore feel your neck is longer.

Elbows The order is 'Elbows out and open'. Push your upper arms slightly away from your sides. Do not lift your arms. Just

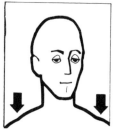

10 'Pull your shoulders towards your feet'

11 'Elbows out and open': position A

12 'Elbows out and open': position B

slide them on their support apart from the body. You are moving at your shoulder joints. Now gently open the angle at your elbows by moving your forearms on their support away from your upper arms.

If you are lying on the floor (in position A) the upper arms and elbows rest on it all the time, and the hands either on tummy or thighs.

If leaning forwards (in position B) your arms move away from your body, and forearms open out at the elbows on the pillows.

If leaning back in the chair (in position C) your upper arms rest across the chair arms, the elbows will be just outside the chair arms with your forearms lying on them. Be sure the fingers also lie on

13 'Elbows out and
open': position C

them and not over the edge. When you feel this position to be
comfortable *stop moving*.

Now recognize the new position by feeling. Realize both arms are
away from your sides and resting on something and that there is an
open angle at the elbows. Do not hurry—*feel*—don't fidget. Concentrate on feeling.

Hands   The order is 'Long'. Keep the heel of your hand
resting where it is and only move your fingers and both thumbs.
Stretch them out to be as long as possible. Go on stretching—feel
them opening out and stiffening and the thumbs stretching away
from the fingers. Extend your wrists upwards if you wish.

Now *stop* and you will feel them lying on the support. Don't bend
them back onto it—just stop stretching and you will find they fall
onto it. So the full order is 'Long—Stop and Supported'.

Now feel those fingers. Notice the pads are resting touching
something, your own body, or the cushion, or the chair arms. Feel
the pads of the fingers touching something, the nails on top and the
fingers separated. Do not allow the fingers to move as you register
the exact texture on which each is resting (p. 65).

Now the thumbs. Can you feel that they too are open and separated from the rest of the hand, resting on a support and quite
heavy? Feel your heavy separated thumbs. Take as long as you like
over this because of the millions of useful messages which you know
are flashing up to your brain giving a clear indication that your
hands are not at work, nor in fear, but in the ease position. Be sure

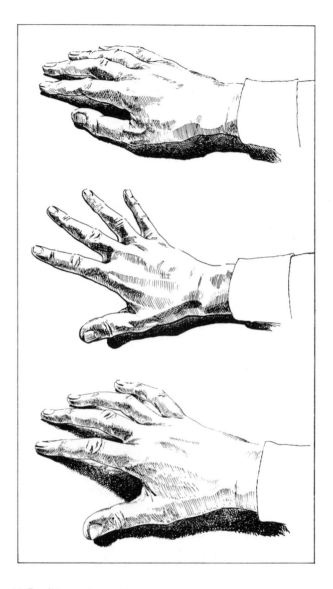

14 Possible starting position for the hands (if not actually clenched)

15 A hand obeying the order to make itself 'long'

16 Fingers and thumbs at rest and supported

you do not allow any little flicking movements while you are recognizing the final positions. Only *feel*.

Please do all that once more, concentrating and moving only the fingers and thumbs. This time I will not help you at all. Do it all using your own feeling to guide you. Do not hurry. Remember the order is 'Long—Stop and Supported'. If the fingers should start to return to a punching position you would feel them scraping along the support.

ORDERS TO THE LEGS

Hips The order is 'Turn your hips outwards'. If in position A and your legs are crossed, uncross and roll the knee caps out to the sides. If in B or C you will feel your knees swing outwards. *Stop.* Now feel this new position at your hips. We do not spend so much time on this as on feeling positions of the fingers and thumbs, because as you remember (p. 20) you have fewer nerves here to convey sensation.

Knees The order is 'Move your knees till they are comfortable' and then *Stop*.

In position A you will probably not want to move your knees at all. In position B and C you ought to adjust the angle at the knees just a little. It is usually quite a small movement of your lower legs forwards or backwards at the knee joints and you will appreciate the feeling when they are comfortable.

Remember it is *your* body. You are in charge, stop when you wish and then feel the comfort in your knees that you selected for yourself. I am not training you, you are training yourself.

Feet and ankles The order is 'Push your feet away from your face'. Do this rather slowly and carefully as some people easily get cramp in the lower leg muscles. (See p. 100).

In position A make your feet bend downwards at the ankles and curl your toes. If in position B and C your heels will rise slightly off the floor and your toes press into it. During this performance you are getting reciprocal relaxation in the muscles on the front of your legs. We want this because the stress position of the feet uses these muscles to keep the feet bending up at the ankle joints, towards the face. In fact when one gives the order 'push your feet away from your face' some people immediately bring them upwards towards the face because quite unconsciously they are accustomed to do this.

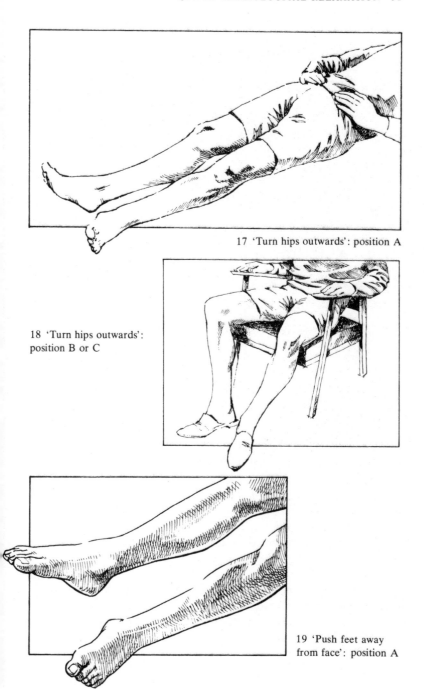

17 'Turn hips outwards': position A

18 'Turn hips outwards':
position B or C

19 'Push feet away
from face': position A

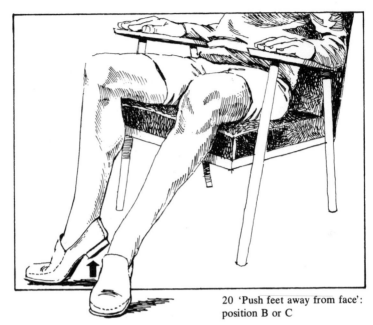

20 'Push feet away from face':
position B or C

If you do, don't worry, you have adopted the tense position from habit; just reverse it and go on doing so while feeling your feet are bending away at the ankle joints. Now *stop*. As you stop you induce relaxation in the muscles on the backs of your legs.

You have now obtained, by yourself, relaxation in all lower leg muscles. *Feel the result.* Your feet are dangling loosely at the ends of your legs in position A, or lying heavily on the floor in position B or C. Notice this is the *result* of chosen activity. Please do not think that, if you tell your feet to dangle loosely, they will do so. They won't. You are too well made. To achieve complete relaxation of the muscles you must produce reciprocal relaxation. Tell the feet to do the actual movement which I have selected for you. Then *stop*. Never confuse an order with a result. They are totally different. Now feel the result—the heavy dangling feet.

Use as much time as you like to enjoy that. There are a great many joints in the feet sending up information to your brain that will help you to feel the result.

Now that you have produced relaxation in the muscles of your arms and legs, just enjoy the sensation of your limbs, lying there where you have arranged them quite immobile—resting at last.

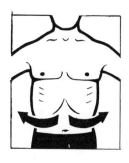

21 Breathing: upper abdomen forward, lower ribs sideways

BREATHING

You really don't need any extra exchange of oxygen and carbon dioxide in your lungs because you are lying or sitting so still that your muscles don't require much. But we do want to make sure that you are using your diaphragm to breathe slowly, low in your chest, and not quickly high up in the narrow area of your chest as tense people usually do. If, after practice, you prefer to put 'Breathing' after 'Body' and 'Head', do so.

I will explain briefly what you have to do and then you perform it yourself, in your own time, keeping it as slow as possible, twice or at most three times. A fuller description of breathing, including the mechanism of the chest is given in Chapter 6 p. 92.

You should breathe in and out through the nose because inside it is so arranged that it warms and filters the air passing through.[5]

Now think about your lower ribs and the triangular area enclosed in front between the curve of your lower ribs on either side and your waist below. As you breathe in, this area gently expands forwards and to either side, slightly lifting your ribs out sideways like the wings of a bird. As you do so the air will flow into and through your nose to fill up your lungs. You have been using your diaphragm but you will not be able to feel its movement as you do not have any suitable sensory nerves there to inform you. Obviously also you cannot feel it by touch as it lies entirely inside your ribs. But you will feel the result of its work as a slight increase of pressure in your abdomen, and in the rib movement.

Never hold your breath but when you are ready, breathe out slowly and easily, not for unduly long. You will feel your ribs fall inwards and downwards again.

All this should be done without any effort. Do not sniff the air in with any force or blow it out. There is no need for huffing and puffing. All you have to do is to give a little extra attention to the area just above your waist in front and to the movements of your ribs which you can readily feel. The exquisitely designed mechanism of your chest will then do the work for you. Never push the lower curve of your abdomen forwards as this is a trick movement performed by arching the spine and interferes with the mechanism.

Don't overdo the breathing even if you are enjoying it. You may upset the respiratory centre in your lower brain whose job it is to regulate your breathing by the amount of carbon dioxide in your blood. Don't annoy it.

ORDERS TO THE BODY

The order is 'Push your body into the support'. You consciously push your whole body into the floor in position A, or onto the table in position B or against the chair back in position C. Now *stop*. Feel that support holding your weight. Notice that you are not to imagine you are falling through it, or floating above it. Use the very acute senses you possess, and feel the whole of your body slumped on that support. You will be registering this by skin pressure. A very common habit of all busy people when they either sit or lie down is then to remain tensed, ready to spring up again for further action. So *feel* your body lying there because you have transferred its weight to a support competent to sustain it.

ORDERS TO THE HEAD

The order is 'Push your head into the support'. That will be the same direction in which you pushed your body. Don't use the words 'backwards' or 'forwards' for some day you will probably wish to lie on your front or your side. 'Push into the support' will always be suitable and the support will receive your head. It is about 10-12 lbs. in weight (nearly a stone of potatoes or 5 kilograms). It is really very heavy to be held on the top of your slender neck with its seven joints. So until your brain is convinced by feeling that your head is supported, some muscles all around this column remain active to prevent your head falling. When you feel the head thoroughly supported *stop* pushing. Now, feel that support holding your heavy head for you. You will probably find this most comforting. Enjoy the relief.

ORDERS TO THE FACE

Mouth   The order is 'Drag your jaw (i.e. your chin) downwards'. Keep your lips closed or your mouth gets dry. Separate your lower teeth from your top teeth and slowly pull the jaw *down*. Feel as it happens. When your teeth are comfortably separated and you feel your heavy jaw hanging inside your mouth, *stop*.

Now feel the slackness of your lips and savour this feeling as much as you can. You remember its multiple nerves (p. 35) that will inform your brain very thoroughly that you are now at ease. So take plenty of time. You may also feel the stretching of the skin of your cheeks. Is your tongue fixed to the roof of your mouth? If so, it is in the stress position; gently loosen it and make it lie in the middle of your mouth. As you do so you may feel your gullet slacken. Take your time, feel your tongue loose in your mouth, touching your lower teeth.

Eyes   Your eyes may already have closed because your brain has told them to do so. It has by now been inundated with messages of ease from joints all over your body and therefore realizes you are having a rest. This is very satisfactory. If your eyes are open the order is 'Close your eyes'.

This, like every other order must be carried out in a precise manner. You lower the upper lids down over the eyes, and that is all you do. You do not screw up the muscles around the eyes at all. It is like pulling a linen blind down over a window—nothing else happens in the face. When the lids are closed do not allow any flickering or blinking. Sometimes this is difficult, so if your eyelids do flap up and down a little don't worry. In time they will learn to stay down.

22 Direction of movement of jaw, eyelids, forehead and scalp

Stop movement and *feel* the result. The result is darkness. This is very pleasurable but don't let your mind wander off into a daze. Enjoy this darkness you have contrived and of which you have complete control. Realize what a long awaited rest you are giving the part of your brain connected with sight. Not only is it not seeing anything, it is not having to decide what action is therefore implied. It really is off duty.

If you should find this darkness at all frightening—some people do at first—open your eyes but don't move anywhere else. If you would rather not close your eyes at all, don't. It is quite a big step to close your eyes consciously if you have never really relaxed fully previously. You may feel rather defenceless at first but soon when you feel safe although relaxed you will be ready to enjoy it. Don't hurry, take your time. When you do you will be quite proud of having achieved the feeling of your eyelids floating lightly on your eyes, complete darkness, and an expressionless face. It is also a real beauty treatment.

Forehead Before you try to smooth this I want to explain that there is a large thin muscle enclosing your head just under your scalp. This is called *occipito frontalis* and extends from your eyebrows to the lower part of your skull at the back. It is like a large close-fitting cap, which gets smaller when it contracts.

When one is tensed and the shoulders rise upwards towards the ears, a spill-over of contraction spreads into this muscle and it often shortens and tightens onto the skull. People who have frequent bouts of tension describe the sensation as 'a tight band round the head', 'a tight hat' or 'a fearful crushing headache'.[6] This is often associated with migraine.

It is difficult to relax this muscle as it does not control any joint. Neither does it have any opposite muscle that would assist us. However, we have left it to the last, so we may be getting a helpful overspill of relaxation in it from the rest of the face, just as it can get an unhelpful overspill of contraction from the neck and shoulder muscles during tension.

So try this. Begin to think of this area just above your eyebrows—don't lift these upwards—and think of smoothing up into your hair, over the top of your head, and down to the back of your neck: rather like a roll-top desk being rolled back. Of course this is difficult. The very difficulty will make you realize how impossible it is to tell muscles to relax, and how much we depend on joints for sensation. You may, however, feel your hair move. Try to think of this smoothing once or twice.

You have now completed the course around the body and I hope you find yourself comfortable and enjoying a sensation of ease which you will recognize as Total Relaxation. If you don't, repeat the course starting at your shoulders. This is an easy progression from the last movement.

YOUR MIND

Sometimes when the body is disciplined into quietude, the mind becomes more active. If so, you must then discipline your mind and not allow it to go off on its own and possibly present you with worrying thoughts which might cause tension all over again. So choose what you allow yourself to think about, just as we chose the orders carefully to give to your body.

You have a wide choice. You can go over the sequence again rather more quickly giving the exact order, then stopping, then feeling the result all around the body. Be sure you always actually perform a small movement.[7] Don't just think about it. Do it. The most important phase, remember, is feeling what is happening and the result in the changed position.

Or you may prefer to leave your body lying perfectly relaxed, and occupy your mind with something quite different. Please select deliberately something that has continuity like a song or poem or prayer that you like. It could be a multiplication table, but do not try to dwell on one thing like a vase of flowers. This is hard work. You just want to keep the thoughts moving gently. You might prefer to remember some happy sequence in the past like swimming or walking along a seashore or through a wood or a shop. Don't plan for the future and if a worry intrudes, ignore it and force your mind to continue thinking along the pleasant path you had chosen.

ENJOYMENT

It is important to spend some time enjoying the result of all your work. The physiologists tell us that whatever gives us pleasure is registered in the brain and the body will ask us to repeat it. Of course we know this to be true in our own experience. The body asks us not only for a drink when it is thirsty. It will tell us exactly the kind of food or drink, which, having already experienced, it prefers at any given moment, including details like how much sugar to put in our tea.

In the same way we can train ourselves by the enjoyment of the result of the physiological relaxation technique. The body will inform us, not only when we are tense and need to change to ease but exactly where the tense positions are, and how badly we are affected by them.

For example we may only be making a slight punching movement with one hand or we may be gripping so hard that the nails are pressing into the palms of both hands. Immediately this can be recognized by the brain and it will ask you to assume the pleasurable state of the ease positions in the hands because you have done this so often before, and registered how much more comfortable it was.[8]

So please really enjoy your present state of total relaxation which you produced in your *own body* by your *own work*. If you are lying on the floor and you wish to change your position, do so. Just roll over into any position you prefer and run through the orders as before. You will find they fit any position you care to use. Do not be afraid to change any position for another, thinking that you will then lose your relaxation. You just retake it in the new position.

USE OF THE METHOD

Now you know what to do to achieve complete relaxation. You have experienced the peace in your own body, and possibly if you are working with someone else, you have watched them achieve it. This is useful, and easy to see, by noticing the positions and the inert look of the limbs, and the fact that the head has made a large dent in the pillow by its weight, the easy breathing, and the lack of any expression on the face. There is no movement anywhere, except a slight movement in the chest. The relaxed person may give a deep sigh from time to time, or drift into sleep.

It is for you to decide what you want to do on any occasion. You may want a slow deep relaxation leading to sleep. Or you may have only a short time at your disposal for rest, so you compose yourself in whatever position you find suitable, go through the technique, and then spend the remainder of the time conscious and relaxed.

Always stretch your limbs and your body in various directions, and yawn if you can, as you sit up before returning to activity. Remember your blood pressure will have dropped, your pulse will be slower and your circulation will have slackened, so give them an opportunity to recover suitable pace, before you stand up and walk away.

The other equally important way to use your new skill, is to feel when any area of your body is adopting the tense positions while you are at work or busy socially and to try and change it to ease without stopping the main activity. Of course it depends on what the activity may be. Sometimes you can change the tense positions almost completely, sometimes only partially. For example during the writing of this book I have often felt tension spreading all over me. I would then lean back in my chair, until my body and head were supported, and put my left arm and hand into full ease positions. I would adjust my legs and sigh out an easy breath. Meanwhile I continued writing with my right hand.

Of course tension tends to creep back again when what one is doing seems important. But it can be monitored if you train yourself to do so. If I am driving a car or lecturing and discover tension spreading, I only use the technique partially. In the former I find it useful to change body, breath and jaw. In the latter, especially shoulders, hands and an easy breath out during a pause. These changes still allow me to give full attention to what I am really doing. Some tension will remain and in these situations is needed. There is plenty of time to get rid of this afterwards.

So you will learn in your daily routine—whatever it may be—when and how much tension must be controlled or eliminated. Remember it is *your* body and *your* tension. It should be under the control of *your* will. But if you sometimes fail, as we all do, don't blame yourself, just go on practising. It's worth it. You will certainly find your facility increasing as time goes on.

CHECK LIST OF ORDERS

ARMS

Shoulders

Order: Pull your shoulders towards your feet. STOP
Result: Feel your shoulders are further away from your ears. Your neck may feel longer.

Elbows

Order: Elbows out and open. STOP
Result: Feel your upper arms away from your body and the wide angle at your elbows. The weight of both arms should be resting on floor, chair arms, or pillow.

Hands

Order: Fingers and thumbs long and supported. STOP
Result: Feel your fingers and thumbs stretched out, separated, and touching support, nails on top. Especially feel your heavy thumbs.

LEGS

Hips

Order: Turn your hips outwards. STOP
Result: Feel your thighs rolled outwards. Kneecaps face outwards.

Knees

Order: Move slightly until comfortable if you wish. STOP
Result: Feel the resulting comfort in your knees.

Feet

Order: Push your feet away from your face, bending at the ankle. STOP
Result: Feel your dangling heavy feet.

BODY

Order: Push your body into the support. STOP
Result: Feel the contact of your body on the support.

HEAD

Order: Push your head into the support. STOP
Result: Feel the contact of your head on the support or
pressure on the pillow.

BREATHING

Choose rate but try to keep it slow. Choose placing in
routine before or after body and head, or when you feel
your breathing rate slowing down. *Breathe in gently.*
Expand the area in front above the waist, and between
the angles of the rib cage, and raise your lower ribs
upwards and outwards like the wings of a bird. Then
breathe out gently. Feel your ribs fall downwards and
inwards. Repeat once or at most twice.

FACE

Jaw

Order: Drag your jaw downwards. STOP
Result: Feel your separated teeth, heavy jaw, and loose
lips— especially your lips.

Tongue

Order: Press your tongue downwards in your mouth.
STOP
Result: Feel your loose tongue and slack gullet.

Eyes

Order: Close your eyes. STOP
Result: Feel your upper lids resting gently over your
eyes, without any screwing up around the eyes. Enjoy
the darkness.

Forehead

Order: Begin above eyebrows and think of smoothing
gently up into your hair, over the top of your head and
down the back of your neck. STOP
Result: Feel your hair move in the same direction.

MIND

Order: Either repeat the above sequence around the
body, possibly more quickly. *Or* choose some subject

which you will enjoy thinking about, and which has a sequence (song, prayer, poem, multiplication table, etc.). *Or* relive some past personal happy occasion. Let the mind play over these thoughts effortlessly, just to keep it occupied.

Return to full activity

Always stretch limbs and body in all directions and yawn. Do not hurry. Sit up slowly and wait for a minute or two before standing up.

TAKING A CLASS

Have a carpeted floor or mats and one pillow for each person's head, plus a few extra. If possible have some upright chairs and tables on which are two pillows. Have some chairs with tall backs and arms. Let each person choose his position (pp. 44, 45). Have the members of the class scattered on the floor and chairs. Never let them lie in rows. They should feel separated, so that they can concentrate on their own body and actions.

Ask the class to demonstrate tense positions they have felt in themselves or seen in others. You will find they will describe the tense positions as on pp. 26, 27. Explain that this is what they will learn to replace with positions of ease.

Explain the action of reciprocal relaxation (p. 39) and therefore the choice of orders. Explain 'order, stop, feel'. Demonstrate clenched hand changing to 'Long and supported'. Explain sensation to brain from joints and skin, not muscles. Then teach Mitchell method as on pp. 46–57.

Part II

5   Keys, Triggers, and Habits

Beyond a wholesome discipline be gentle with yourself.
St Paul's Church, Baltimore 1692

KEYS

A key position is the term I give to the joint change that unlocks tension and that a person finds easiest to do. It will be quite different for different people. Sometimes it is the straightening out of the fingers and thumbs that brings almost instant relief and starts off the other joint changes which the person can feel spreading over the body. Sometimes the pushing back of the head, or the easy outward breath may be the key to the other ease changes.

Find out for yourself which change is the simplest, that you always get right the first time, and where the sensation of the changed joints is easiest to appreciate. Dwell on this sensation, practise the change quickly and then slowly. Savour the whole movement as it happens and when it ends. Gradually you will deepen your appreciation of what is happening and your actual joint change will become very much quicker and the feeling more acute.

The more you enhance this as you practise the movement the more use your key position will become to you. A tennis player practises his best stroke just as much as his others, because he knows that it is with that stroke he is going to win his match. Your key position is going to be your winning movement in your fight to prevent unwanted muscular tension dominating you.

A wine taster isn't just satisfied when he can taste the difference between white wine and red. By persistently training his own appreciation of taste he will become able to differentiate not only between districts but between vineyards and years. The tennis player is training his body response to orders from the brain. The wine taster is training the appreciation in his brain in response to sensation in his body.

Your appreciation of exact joint and skin sensation can be increased enormously by repeated practice and application. Just try. You will find your key position will really become a weapon you instinctively use to prevent muscular tension gaining on you when you react to some annoyance or fear or worry.[1]

When you are practising your key position you may find it helpful to talk aloud, saying what you feel in the joints as the changes take place. Be sure you do not add anything fanciful—say only what you actually feel. Then if you are not sure if you have achieved all that is possible, compare it with the description in Chapter 4. In fact you will in time get much more interesting information from your own experience than it is possible to suggest when generalising here.

Suppose it were the hands that were your key, your talk might be something like this for each hand practised:

'I can feel my four fingers are straight and separated at the knuckles (the joints where the fingers meet the hand). When I then register the further two joints in each finger in turn, I can feel each joint is nearly straight. It is certainly not curled with the finger tips in towards the palm. Indeed if I stretch out the fingers actively a little bit more I can feel them straightening further and the skin on the underside of these joints being definitely stretched. Now I stop stretching the fingers and I feel the skin slacken and the finger tips on the support. Now I give all my attention to the finger tips. I am not going to move the fingers in any way. I am simply going to register the texture of what they are lying on.'

If you are lying on your back on the ground wearing shirt and trousers it is possible for you to have each of your four finger tips resting on a different texture—the fabric of your shirt, the shell of a button on your shirt, the fabric of your trousers, and the leather of the belt that holds the trousers up. See if you can recognize these four different textures under the spread out four fingers. There is no need to feel silly concentrating on this, you will need much more attention to learn how to type or to hold the different kinds of golf clubs correctly. So work often at it—it will pay dividends in the board room, in the broadcasting studio or indeed on the golf course.

Practise away at your key position and as you become more adept both at changing and feeling you will gain confidence that you really will be able to prevent tension building up (see pp.33-36). You will have a great sense of victory the first few times you achieve this; after that you will expect it.

The opposite of the key positions of course are those which you are worst at. These too should be practised separately but for a different reason. These will be the positions that have been personal and habitual to you in moments of strain and will therefore be more difficult to reverse.

I told you, for example, that on giving the order 'Push your feet away from your face' some people immediately bend their feet up at the ankles. Also some people find difficulty changing their arm positions and bend them up across their bodies because that was their long standing habit. Do not blame yourself, do not blame your body. It was perfectly correct to defend itself by this primitive reflex in moments of anxiety. You are going to teach your body a better way. But you must regard your own body as you would a puzzled child learning a new skill. Be gentle with yourself. I have seen people swearing away because the whole body wouldn't obey immediately at the first time of asking.

Above all enjoy what you are doing, enjoy the change to the ease position. Expect your body to help you. Don't drive it. Pleasure is one of the most helpful ways of learning anything. Since you are teaching your body a soothing technique, it is generally easy to feel pleasure while practising physiological relaxation.

When I am lecturing on the subject I like, if the audience is small, e.g. a hospital staff, to have facilities for them to lie on the floor to perform the technique after I have described it. When they have finished and have sat up again I never can resist saying 'Did you enjoy it?' and I am left in no doubt by the replies that, in general, although it was their first performance, they did. So you see I am not asking you to do the impossible. Joint change to ease is possible and is pleasurable.[2] Seek out your key positions and your most difficult ones and by practice you will achieve control. Control of one will help the other (see 'Habits', p. 69).

TRIGGERS

'I get exhausted at meetings' said the vicar I was treating for tension.

'Why, what happens?'

'The Bishop never stops twiddling his pastoral ring on his finger. It nearly drives me mad.'

'What exactly does he do?'

The vicar then placed the fingers of his left hand around the ring finger of his right hand and gave a very exact demonstration of how the Bishop twiddled his ring. He had obviously made a minute study of the performance.

Now whether there is some deep psychological significance in the effect of the ring, I do not know. The fact remains that he knew to a nicety the trigger that set off the tension that exhausted him. Yet he kept on activating that trigger by gluing his eyes on what annoyed him. This is exactly what so many of us do.

I suggested to the priest that he do three things.

1. Stop watching the agitating ring.

2. Use his key position first and then try and change himself into the ease positions as much as possible without making it obvious to others.

3. Form this into a habit.

The moment he found himself noticing the ring he was to avert his eyes to some object of his choice in the room and concentrate on it while he changed his hands to the 'long and supported' position (p. 48) which was his key position. He was to do this often so that it became a habit.

The sight of the ring then became the trigger for ease positions rather than for the tense positions. The only outward sign of this activity would be that he looked happier. Later on the vicar told me he had ceased to be exhausted at these meetings and had begun to enjoy them.

So try to find your trigger situations and trigger people. We all have them—people that drive us mad—Mrs So and So is so stupid—I can't stand people with red hair—the very sight of that man infuriates me—I hate washing the dishes—making the beds—gardening—committee meetings—interviewing applicants for job vacancies—washing the car. Their name is legion.

Think it all out carefully. Think of what 'gets on your nerves' as triggers of tension, and decide how you can circumvent them. Maybe you can find a boy scout to wash the car—many people do. Maybe you can swop chores you hate with another member of the family who has another hate that doesn't trigger you off into the jitters. You may even enjoy doing it and then find it becomes a hobby. Every sensitive person needs a hobby. Indulge yourself in it and tensions disappear.

One good idea is to label some of your trigger situations; here's how:

Have a coloured tab on your watch, kitchen or office clock and on your telephone, so that every time you look at the time or lift the telephone to make or take a call you are reminded to use your key position. It's amazing how much of a threat these inanimate objects can be. Don't let them tense you up.

I used to ask my postnatal patients to fix some artificial flowers or a framed map in their lavatory, the strangeness of which would remind them to perform their exercises, if they decided to make this association in their minds. Everyone else would accept them as part of the decor.

And as for that stupid or overbearing or not-to-be trusted Mr or Mrs So and So, you know they have those odd ways so do not let yourself get surprised and tense every time they are displayed. Use your intelligence to be prepared for what's going to happen and maybe someone else will be wearing something that you find amusing or interesting to look at. There's always an alternative to focus on, something to defuse you, if you seek for it. Don't be triggered into primitive reaction against your better judgment. Use that judgment to recognize your triggers and decide how to change them or if that is not possible to elude them. Yes, I said 'Elude'. Don't make it a question of pride to go through with some annoying performance which does no-one any good. Evasion is wiser than stress; sometimes it is wiser to resign from the committee or to send your junior to the business conference.

I remember once being held up in a queue of cars. We stopped every few yards, waited some minutes, then went slowly ahead and stopped again. Suddenly the door of the car two ahead of me burst open, a man shot out of it and ran to the driver of the car immediately ahead of me. As he ran he began taking off his jacket and when he reached the window of the car he began to shout and put up his fists and was obviously asking the driver to come out and fight. Luckily the man didn't respond to the invitation, and at that moment the cars began to move forward and the angry man had to dash back to his car to keep up with the queue.

Whatever could have triggered off that unfortunate man to behave so irrationally and make such a spectacle of himself? Surely nothing the other driver could have done would merit such a display of anger? Yet when even a small trigger is repeatedly activated in difficult circumstances tension can get quite out of control. In the following chapter I shall deal with many of the triggers often present when driving a motor car.

So notice your triggers and deal with them before they create the tension that gets beyond your control. You will do this partly by thinking the issues through and by planning, and partly physically by using your key position and then working through the other body orders in Chapter 4. Growing muscular tension must only get the chance to spread if you intend to use it for action. Controlled anger is suitable on certain occasions. But you ought to be able to choose whether you allow yourself to get angry or not, and you should always remain in control of your anger.

Sometimes the build-up of tension is not caused by a repetition of one particular trigger that happens to affect you and that can be identified and dealt with. It may be a succession of small happenings each insignificant but the cumulative effect of which would annoy anyone. The alarm clock doesn't work, the bath water is cold, the toast is flaccid, the bus is late, the office lift isn't working, the secretary is off ill and there is a massive, nasty post.

By 11 a.m. any normally reactive man or woman is ready to swear, scream or kick something. But if you can (a) recognize the accumulation of triggers and use your common sense, either to side step or deal with these conditions, (b) use your skill at physiological relaxation and (c) still keep on working, you are well on the way to doubling your salary, and prolonging your working life. You'll be happier than by allowing yourself to get submerged under a growing load of reactive tension. Cut through it as it develops. Never let it spread.

Later, when you quietly assess the annoyances of the day, you may well come to the conclusion that there are pretty easy answers to prevent a recurrence:

1.   Get an alarm clock that works.
2.   Fix the thermostat on the water heater or get an instantaneous heater.
3.   Make your own toast on a pop-up toaster.
4.   Get a bike or an earlier bus.
5.   Regard that walk upstairs as a bonus not a bore and decide to repeat it.

Then you will be able to cope with the post without your secretary.

HABITS

We all have them and a good thing too. It saves such a lot of unnecessary thinking. Now I am not trying to be an amateur psychiatrist but I do suggest that you review some of your habits from the point of view of triggers and keys as described in this chapter. Remember, habits are not like reflex actions which are innate. Habits have always been built up by repetition through the conscious brain and therefore can be changed at will.

HOME

Housewives often have numerous triggers for tension in the arrangement or lack of it in the lay-out of their kitchens. Can you stand in one spot and make a cup of tea or coffee? Can you prepare vegetables, chop them up, get rid of the waste, and put them on the stove without moving from a stool? None of this is difficult to arrange. It simply means having all the implements and ingredients necessary grouped around, on the wall or just above eye level at the appropriate spot. Yet in how many kitchens can one do this? How often instead do you see people walking about, or bending down and up—that most tiring of actions—to find things they may use several times a day.[3]

Have you done away with all cupboards below hip level and changed then to drawers that can be pulled out and the contents easily seen? Or have you had hanging baskets fixed on the inside of the cupboard doors so that, as they swing open, they reveal their contents?

Everything you use often should be to hand at eye level or just above—never below. It is amazing how often some people walk across their kitchen for the salt, or a favourite knife, or to a rubbish bin, when with a little thought and planning they could have all requirements beside the place where they are usually used. The salt and pepper mills for example just above the cooking stove and the stirring spoons etc. hanging on hooks near.

No wonder some people hate cooking and get all tense when they have to do it. They tell you 'It makes me tired just to think about it'. They may come to dislike it so much that they refuse to think about it, or about the layout of their kitchen, and just continue with their old time and energy-consuming habits in conditions that would never be permitted in any factory—the time and motion boys would never allow it. Ergonomics is the name of the science we are talking about. It means making the job suitable for the worker and teaching him how to perform it without muscular or other strain. It is a recognized necessity for happy, healthy and efficient workers.

You are the best judge of your kitchen habits, for you only know how much, and how often, and for what purposes, your kitchen is used. But do give it some thought and prevent your tensions and tiredness before they arise and then accumulate.

In the home the other job causing most tension appears to be bedmaking. I think any money spent on duvets that dispense with all top sheets, blankets and eiderdowns would be well spent. In the long run of course they save money as there is less laundry to be done. If you prefer weight you can always add a rug on top.

On the other hand some tension-making habits are not caused by things but by personal attitude. Some housewives need to learn to give up the burden of perfection which they have inflicted on themselves. Think about it.

OFFICE

Secretaries and typists should also inspect the tools of their trade—the chair, table, typewriter, files and other office equipment that they have to use frequently. These should all be suitable in height and placing for the person and work involved, otherwise strain and tension will result. Examine your chair and be sure it fits you. Especially see that it is stable. Too often they rock about, which may cause strain.

Consider the length of time spent sitting continuously and try to use your ease joint changes frequently. Try to intersperse sitting periods with walking ones.[4] There is usually filing or other jobs to be done. If these are interspersed throughout the sitting period, so much the better for the circulation, posture, muscular control and breathing of the secretary. Tension is often prevented by switching from one job to another and then returning refreshed to the first. On p. 74 a technique which may help you when telephoning is suggested. You will also find hints on public speaking and interviews in the same chapter.

Sometimes a sudden change of work habit may be thrust upon us. This can be disastrous for some people, especially if it be part of promotion in office or factory. Sometimes this involves new time schedules, different type of work, change of place and or companions. All this should be considered before accepting the change. No increase of money or prestige is worth the sacrifice of habits that suit us in exchange for a routine that may destroy us by stress.

BEAUTY AND SEX DIFFICULTIES

If you look in a mirror when you are feeling troubled and therefore tense, you will probably see a wrinkled forehead, lowering brows, pursed up mouth, and possibly the teeth grinding together. This last can often be seen as a continuous movement in the joint of the jaw bone just in front of the ear. You may also feel your tongue clamped to the roof of your mouth. Is this the face you are in the habit of showing to your family and friends?

Try changing all this consciously (Chapter 4 p. 55) and watch smoothness and any beauty you may possess spread over your face. Better for you and much pleasanter for those whom you meet. Make this change a habit.

Specialists in sexual disorders such as frigidity in women, premature ejaculation, or impotence in men, have often said that to have control of tension is a first essential in the cure of such distressing disabilities.

I suggest anyone so suffering make use of physiological relaxation as part of their recovery programme.

Many women have told me how helpful they have found the technique when they have shown signs of the well known premenstrual syndrome (P.M.S.). The woman becomes moody, she is accident prone, and indeed, emergency admissions to hospitals increase. She is more sensitive to pain and depression, the threshold to both diminishing. It is therefore obvious that to be able to relax under one's own control, in such circumstances, is both reassuring and helpful.

DISPLACEMENT ACTIVITY

This is perhaps the place to mention an interesting phenomenon of the animal world, which throws much light on our more or less attractive 'personal habits'. Animals are as much subject to the fear reflex as we are, and it has been noted that they have a number of activities which they substitute for fight or flight. Birds when facing up to each other in some territory squabble, will suddenly poke and preen their feathers. Furry creatures have bouts of licking and hairy ones scratch. It's the same with us: our 'displacement activities', as they are called, include lip biting, nose picking and powdering, nail biting, thumb sucking (smoking), teeth grinding, gum chewing, hair smoothing and scratching, cuff shooting, skirt smoothing, change jingling—and so on.[5]

As alternatives to the positions of stress catalogued at the end of Chapter 2, maybe we should tolerate, if not welcome, these manifestations in ourselves. On the other hand, they do on occasion lead to self-disgust and often can act as triggers to tension for other people who have to watch us. If we want to, it's a simple matter to replace them, once recognized, with our key change, into physiological relaxation. It's a substitute which will give the body equal or better satisfaction.

There really seems to be little point in trying to relax yourself out of tension, if that tension need never have been created in the first place, and is going to be repeated again and again in preventable circumstances. What a waste of energy. Prevention is always better than cure.

Just as we can learn new skills, so throughout life we can learn habits or lose them if we really wish to do so enough. It is interesting that the Alexander technique for body control, which is well known in England and America, is entirely based on changing muscular habits.[6] Behaviour therapy, a branch of para-medicine which has been very popular in recent years, is also based on habit changing. The patient is taught to substitute another routine for one which is preventing him from leading a normal life. Part of the Behaviour Therapists' routine is to tell their patients to relax before carrying out further instructions.

Patients suffering from agoraphobia (fear of open spaces) and other distressing habit phobias have told me that by learning physiological relaxation they were relieved of their symptoms. Migraine sufferers also seem to be helped.

Examine and get rid of tension-creating habits wherever possible. Then you won't have used up all your energy on unnecessary muscle work and you will be fresher to deal with what can't be foreseen. For these occasions I hope you will be ready to use your own physiological keys to control any developing tension. Habits become part of ourselves. They must be treated with respect and selected with care. Don't let them just envelop you willy nilly like a mist on a moor.

6   Application of Technique

I have tried to give general directions as to how this physiological relaxation technique may be used, and fitted into daily patterns of life. If time and place allow it can be used fully for complete rest, or frequent variable single joint changes can prevent tension spreading while still at work. There are, however, some special circumstances, and particular applications of it which I would like to mention as well.

1. Telephoning
2. Interviews, speech making or broadcasting
3. Driving
4. Insomnia
5. Helping the ill patient
6. Breathing difficulties
7. Antenatal, labouring and postnatal mothers
8. Osteo-arthritis of the neck and lower spinal column
9. Psychiatric patients

TELEPHONING

Many people spend hours a day on the telephone and have often told me how exhausting they find it. When I asked them to show me their telephoning technique, after they had got over what they thought was an idiotic question, it became apparent that it was in fact this—or the lack of it—that was tiring them. Have you noticed the contortions in which some people sit while telephoning? Good technique is worth practising.

Sit in the chair you are accustomed to use for telephoning. If at all possible this chair should have a back tall enough and arms long enough to support your head and arms.[1] Please consider having this kind of chair if you have to do much telephoning. I have often asked a business man or woman or a housewife to change the chair they usually use to one like this. Often they find a suitable one in another room or if they have had to buy one they have found it well worth the money spent, although you may not feel it necessary to have one built to measure as I have known some men to do.

23 Relaxed telephoning

You decide which hand you use to hold the telephone. This will be influenced by whether you are right or left handed and whether you have to make notes while you are telephoning. If so, have the writing pad and pen to hand.

Now sit well back in the chair with both your feet on the ground. You must see that the height of both your chair and desk fits *you*.

Pretend the telephone rings. Do not bend forward to reach it. Stretch out your hand to hold it—remember a tight clutch puts up your blood pressure (p. 28)—at the same time lean back in your chair with your head resting on it and put your other arm on the chair arm in the relaxed position (elbow out and open, fingers long and supported).

When you are gently holding the telephone, lift it to your ear and if possible, rest the elbow on the arm of the chair on that side, or if this isn't possible try to rest the weight of your arm on the back of your chair. Before you say anything take an easy breath low in your chest.

What you are trying to prevent is that hunched up ready-to-spring position over the telephone, when you grasp it as though it were trying to escape, while your other hand grips a pen or, even worse, holds a cigarette.

24 Relaxed telephoning
while notetaking

When you have to write something move the elbow of the arm holding the telephone onto the desk, lean easily forwards to do so and write with your other hand. The writing hand and forearm remain resting on the desk.

As you stop writing, lean back again. These small recurring movements often stop tension building up, and prevent you bawling angrily down the telephone; as your anger grows, your tension strengthens, and your relationships weaken.

Now pretend you are leaning back holding the phone and listening. Run through the relaxation orders for the whole body except the telephone arm. Do this in half a minute. Keeping the eyes open and alert, begin and end with the face changes. These are especially helpful. Do not be afraid that you might look silly with a dragged down chin and smoothed forehead. You will just look more pleasant, and think too how you are quietening your heart and blood pressure instead of allowing them to respond to danger signals as you get tense and worked up. Teach yourself to be comfortable as you listen and reply, and soon it becomes a habit to pull your shoulders down and make the other small joint changes as the conversation proceeds. This is much better than your body getting ready to fight a battle each time the phone rings.

INTERVIEWS, SPEECH MAKING, AND BROADCASTING

These are obvious times for the production of stress positions all over the body, shallow breathing or breath holding, and fidgeting. None of this inspires confidence in yourself or in those watching you.

The aim should be to get rid of the tensions while remaining absolutely alert. This is not simply a matter of relaxation but of combining relaxation and many other things, that build up your own self assurance and so prevent panic. Here are some ways to help to fortify your confidence beforehand.

Preparation and rehearsal of your script, speech headings, or other information that may be necessary for the occasion must be thorough. For broadcasting, practise with a microphone, play it back, and time it with a stop watch. Accustom yourself to flicking your eye from the page to the clock and timing each page. I like to have each page timed with the correct time to finish written in red at the foot of the page. Practise moving pages noiselessly, they should never need to be turned over. If you are to speak extempore whether at an interview, a meeting, or broadcasting, still practise. Verify every detail you intend to mention from the appropriate expert, think out in advance any questions you might be asked, and what you would hope to reply, being generous with information. This is only fair to your audience; the more you are considering their feelings the less you can think of your own. Complete absorption in your audience, seen or unseen, is the best way of conquering your own tension.

You should take trouble with your appearance, whether you are to be seen or not, and choose well ahead suitable clothes and shoes. All this gives you confidence and helps to prevent nervous tension at the time.

Do you sweat when you are nervous? Then decide to wear something easy at the neck and sleeves and made of cotton or wool, not artificial fibres. If you are a woman a skirt with a wide hem is easier to manage.

Practise sitting in your chosen clothes on a small upright rather uncomfortable chair, which might be the kind allotted to you at the event. Keep your eyes open and your mind completely alert throughout. Sit well back in the chair with both feet on the ground and your head erect. Press your head and body well back, and tense your bottom. This keeps you glued to the chair and gives you a firm foundation so that you remain well in charge of yourself, and therefore of the situation. Now perform tiny adjusting movements of physiological relaxation in all your joints, especially your hands and feet, face and breathing. When waiting to speak keep your lower ribs gently moving sideways, you will then find you cannot hold your breath, which is so common when nervous.

Dragging your jaw downwards and smoothing your forehead upwards at the same time is good preparation for talking. Then as you do all this suddenly say 'one, two, three, four, five, six, seven, eight, nine, ten' very clearly and definitely and you will accustom yourself to breaking into speech while remaining alert yet relaxed. Repeat this several times and listen to your own voice. It should sound as it usually does, absolutely natural, with no extra inflexions or affectations.

Then try saying the days of the week and then the months of the year backwards—'December, November, etc.' and see how your posture and relaxation behave. This is to accustom you to thinking while speaking aloud and at the same time retaining some muscular and relaxation control. Try this especially if you have experienced panic in the past.

On the day, if, in spite of careful rehearsals, you do find yourself making a high pitched strangled noise—just remember you are to carry on talking. The interest of your subject and the influence of your audience will overcome your 'nerves' and you will be able to re-establish your tension control, which you have practised, as you proceed. You will appreciate that some degree of nervous tension is always necessary for any successful public appearance. It helps to 'deliver the goods'.

Finally on the day of the event forget all the preparations, relax thoroughly lying on a comfortable bed, then go and enjoy the adventure of meeting the people who are waiting for you, full of expectation. You won't disappoint them.

DRIVING A MOTOR CAR

The main object—apart from getting to your destination —is to prevent the build-up of tiredness and of tension which in turn leads to more tiredness. Both of these are so often the cause of slight errors of judgment which in certain circumstances can produce a disastrous accident out of all proportion to its origin.

DRIVING WHEN ANGRY

It is of first importance never to start driving immediately after you have had any quarrel or been involved in other incidents giving rise to tension. Don't think you'll get rid of your temper by driving—you are more likely to rid yourself of an arm or leg in some terrible accident.

Please give yourself five minutes before you drive away. This is enough for a quick walk round the block or a garden if you are lucky enough to have one close. Start walking quickly as your temper dictates then gradually slow down if you can and go through all possible joint changes as you continue walking. Let the breath find its own level, except for an exaggeration of the outward sigh when you feel like it.

When you feel the tension of your body receding, when you have pushed the cause of the quarrel into your subconscious and told it to find you a solution which you will expect to receive later, you will feel much more in control of yourself. You are then fit to take control of that lethal weapon, a motor car. Be sure you have a dragged down jaw and your tongue in the middle of your mouth as you drive away. No-one can keep up a temper with a sagging jaw and loose mouth and tongue. Ensure that the hips are firmly back in the seat. Sit upright supported by the seat while leaving the shoulders free. As a motoring safety officer has recently said, 'Relax your body and let your brain do the work'.

SEATING

Plenty has already been written about the importance of having comfort in the driving seat. The seat should be the right height and distance from the pedals so that the knees are slightly bent when the pedals are depressed. The back of the seat should really support your own back—especially at your waist. It is often useful to have a suitable sorbo cushion to sit on and one of the back rests specially designed to fit on car seats. Vary how you use them. You will often find that it gives as much relief to muscle ache to remove one or other or both of these pillows as when you put them in place.

The thing that muscles like best is change, as do the joints of the spine. By altering the way in which the body weight passes through the spinal column, and the buttocks, you get just enough change of posture to alter the strain passing through the muscles and ligaments of your back.

Once you have learned physiological relaxation and so have trained yourself in receiving feeling from all your joints, and you understand about skin contact sending information to your brain, you can put that knowledge to good use. Don't just sit there like a zombie unaware whether your body is comfortable or not. Feel it. Then attend to its needs, varying the position of the seat and seat belt where necessary and also the placing of the cushions. Put your head back on the head rest, shut your eyes and do the shoulder and face changes for a moment. After that you can drive away—a safer person to meet on the road.

THE STEERING WHEEL

You will have been taught to grasp the steering wheel at 10 to 2, or ¼ to 3 (referring to the hands of a clock). It depends on the length of your arms and of your back how far forward this makes you stoop over the wheel and whether you should consider changing your grasp. The ideal position is to have the whole spine supported with the head balanced above and not in front of your neck and to have the weight of the arms balanced so that you have your elbows hanging easily at your sides and your hands holding the wheel comfortably. There is no need to put a stranglehold on it. The thumbs should not grasp around the wheel. A tight hold produces jerky steering and tension. The top picture opposite shows how you should look.

How often instead do we see the posture of desperation.

TRAFFIC LIGHTS AND HOLD-UPS

First use your common sense. Don't fume. Don't blow your horn. It is a forced rest from driving. Use it.

Immediately the car has stopped, put gear into neutral, handbrake on and feet off the pedals, take your hands off the steering wheel onto your lap, put your head back against the head rest if you have one, at the same time doing your body and head, shoulders, face, arms and hands changes. If you are in good practice you will

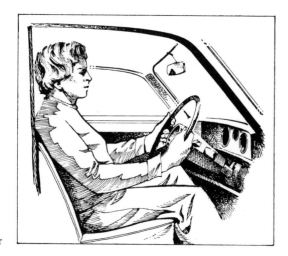

25 The relaxed driver

26 The desperate driver

get completely relaxed in these parts in about a minute. Do not close your eyes because you have to be ready immediately to drive away when the traffic flow starts again. If you can see that you are stuck in a complete holdup, use it as an opportunity to get rid of driving tensions and fatigue. Try turning your head gently from side to side, then tilt your head as far back as you can and then bring it forwards slowly, chin tucked in towards your chest. You will free the seven joints of your neck from the constriction resulting from the need to keep your head facing forwards all the time. The movements hasten the circulation to and from and around your brain. This therefore helps your thinking power.

Then finish with a 'three point pull'.[2] Pressing your chin backwards and keeping your eyes looking straight forwards, try to stretch the top of your head straight upwards; do not tilt it backwards. At the same time pull both your shoulders downwards thus:

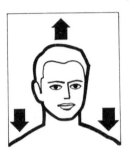

27 The three point pull

This stretches thoroughly all the joints in your neck which tend to be compressed by the weight of your heavy head (5 kilos) pressing down on them. You may well be surprised by a most refreshing feeling that your head is shooting up about two inches (5 cms.). This shows how much you were slouching before without being aware of it. Slouching is tiring. Of course, as you go through this routine, or part of it, you must be ready to move on immediately if the block suddenly clears. Instructors call this 'Intelligent anticipation'. We all know how ready some people are to toot if you appear to hover for a single second.

I have been driving around London for years using these tricks. You will find they keep you rested, yet you never lose control of the car. You just use sensibly the intervals in driving forced upon you. Don't worry that people will think you are crazy. They don't seem to notice. Mostly they are gazing fixedly ahead—tense.

MUSIC AND ROOFS

Some people find music in the car a great help in relieving tension. The one thing I require above all others for town driving is a sunshine roof. I have had one put in every car I have ever owned and the joy of having all the windows shut but fresh air and often sunshine coming cleanly in from above instead of from the surrounding exhausts is, to me, well worth the money.

Think out what luxury in your car will give you continuous pleasure and so cut down tension and *have it*. It's probably cheaper than an accident. I don't mean a cocktail cabinet. Try music—some people like to make their own by whistling or singing—or opening the roof, they are safer.

OTHER DRIVERS

Their behaviour can induce tension which should be cut through as it develops and never allowed to get beyond manageable proportions. The instinctive reaction—and how often one sees it—when another driver cuts in or is otherwise discourteous or annoying is to grasp the wheel as though it were the reins of a runaway horse, increase speed, lean forward, distort the face and probably swear. Tension has begun.

Instead, train yourself to do the body, head, and arm changes immediately: for me the jaw and tongue changes are essential. My tongue leaps to the roof of my mouth and my jaw sets hard on these occasions. It is only when I undo them that I realize how tense and exasperated I was becoming. Of course if you will also prevent yourself trying to retaliate, that is most beneficial to the whole stream of vehicles. I think you will find that if you keep yourself relaxed and comfortable, you really can't be bothered to overtake or block the stupid person who is undoubtedly going to come to a sticky situation sooner or later—make sure you are not part of it.

LONG DISTANCE DRIVING

Keep the car well ventilated at all times. Open windows a bit at the top all round—this keeps air (hot or cold) flowing. Don't try to relax by driving with your arm on the window sill on warm days—it reduces control.

Do consider the length of time you intend to sit continuously at the wheel. For the 'family' driver one to three hours maximum should be the plan. You may think this sounds very impractical but it has been found that it gives better health results rather than driving glued to the seat for many hours. It is also safer. So get out and walk for four minutes—that only means two minutes away from the car and two minutes to return. Swing your arms, do some deep breathing, look around you and enjoy whatever the situation offers—food and drink or a view. A stop at a filling station is another good opportunity to *get out* of the car. Take your mind off the continuous repetitive chore of driving. The activity will get your whole circulation on the go again and relieve strain in continuously tensed-up muscles. On a long journey I know some people drive into a lay-by and have a little sleep. They take a kitchen timer to wake them up. All this means you return to driving refreshed and relaxed and you will easily make up the short time lost because you will be driving so comfortably.

INSOMNIA

Reams have already been written on this subject and the number of cures suggested seems endless. Here are some general tips I have found helpful for patients and some ways of using physiological relaxation as a help to reduce the misery of this trying condition.

Sleeplessness can strike at the beginning of the night or again when we wake up blithe as a robin in the middle of the night and sleep seems a million miles away. If you examine your body pattern at either of these times you will probably find you are completely tense, lying there with clenched fists furiously demanding that sleep should come to you. It is a very natural reaction. We remember we must work tomorrow, then difficulties of home or business come into our mind for attention and before we realize it, we are gripped in the fear-tension reflex which by now you and I can recognize only too well. Sleep becomes more and more unlikely. Let us look at the matter quietly and rationally and probably we can find a way through.

SLEEPLESSNESS AT THE BEGINNING OF THE NIGHT

Are you reasonably physically tired when you want to sleep? If not, find for yourself some suitable exercise beforehand—walking the dog, a run round the garden, etc. Learn by experience how food affects your sleeping—either a full tummy or a moderately empty one will suit you best. Give it what it wants. Some people find a milky drink and a biscuit suits them, others

APPLICATION OF TECHNIQUE 85

prefer whisky or nothing at all. Pamper your tummy.

Is the temperature of the room and of yourself suitable? Don't perpetuate that howling draught from a half open window that used to be considered correct for a bedroom. If you air the room thoroughly during the day you will usually have enough fresh air for the night unless you have central heating turned full on in the bedroom, which in any case is always a bad idea. You are not going to breathe very deeply during sleep—you don't need vast quantities of fresh air. There is nothing virtuous about lying in a draught. Yet I have known people brag about their open windows while their bronchitis got steadily worse. In summer, if you want open windows, always open them wide. It is the narrow slit that causes the draught on your neck or chest.

In summer sleeping naked between cotton sheets instead of in bed clothes and sheets of artificial fibre will often bring sleep, while in winter, a safe electric blanket, or hot water bottle, bed socks or extra woollies may just bring that little extra bit of comfort that will tip the scale into sleep rather than wakefulness. I presume you have already chosen the mattress that suits you and also the weight of bedclothes. Don't skimp your spending on these. Remember you probably spend about a third of your life in bed.

Examine your pattern of joint position as by now you are used to doing. You will probably find it is not the ease pattern, so having adjusted your pillows and position to what you usually like in bed, start going through the changes in any position you like. The orders which you have memorized will fit any position. Don't use your 'key'. Begin at the shoulders and follow the whole routine. Only make very small movements, just enough to get the stretch on the working tensed muscles, and dwell as long as you can on the resulting ease feelings in the joints. Keep repeating the whole sequence around your body.

As you quieten down your muscles and breathing from tension into ease, what you are aiming at is bodily comfort and mental boredom. You know how one's mind races along during sleeplessness and the best way to drive out the worrying thoughts is by replacing them with boring ones. Concentrate deeply on the position of each joint as it changes into the ease position. Surely nothing could be more boring than thinking about the shape of your ankle joints. But you really have to work quite hard concentrating to control and direct your thoughts. It is this concentrating which is so important to cut through the continuation of disturbing thoughts. If, in the middle of all this performance, you feel like changing position, perhaps rolling onto your other side, just do so. Then begin again on your joint changes, do the sequence fairly quickly and dwell on the ease feelings. You will feel your breathing change of its own accord.

At some point your boredom may be gaining nicely and the worrying thoughts receding. Then you may want to change to some religious meditation, or to poetry reciting, garden or menu planning, etc. Some people like to keep on repeating just one word of their choice. If worrying thoughts intrude again go back at once to the physiological relaxation changes, and production of boredom. Soon I hope you will find comfort in your body and mind and that feeling of withdrawing from reality that precedes sleep.

WAKING IN THE MIDDLE OF THE NIGHT

Once you realize you are properly awake, get out of bed. If you awoke feeling hot put the covers back to air the bed or turn over the duvet and pillow. If you awake cold put something extra on the bed and turn on the bed heater. Of course, if you are sharing a bed you will just have to deal with your side of it. Now go to the lavatory and empty your bladder, don't just lie in bed and wonder if you want to go—get up. On the way back call in the kitchen and fetch yourself something to eat and drink. Not much, just a little something easy to pick up. It depends on your diet of the moment what you choose—some like a banana or a biscuit and others a piece of chocolate or glass of milk. If you have a guilty feeling that your dentist would disapprove, include a slice of apple to finish with.

Bring your loot back to bed which by now will be at a new comfortable temperature. Read some fairly soothing book and slowly eat your takings from the kitchen. Of course, if you live in a vast mansion and the kitchen isn't handy, you will have to see there is a box of goodies and a small thermos of your favourite drink in your bedroom. Now you can put out the light and settle down in your most comfortable position to do your physiological relaxation changes as mentioned at the beginning of this section.

All this will have taken about six to ten minutes and soon you should be back in deep sleep. It is much better to have a positive routine like this than to thresh about the bed uncomfortable and

APPLICATION OF TECHNIQUE 87

cross and getting nowhere, perhaps for hours. The little prize of something to eat is very comforting and that is better than getting angry with yourself. It also diverts some blood to your stomach to digest it and so probably you have less blood in your brain to think with. Soothe yourself by all these tricks and then swamp your brain with boredom.

Suppose you wake with the worry of some half-done business, or job to do—a letter to write or a child's school uniform to iron. Get up and complete it, if it is work that will take you half an hour. If it is going to be longer, just get it prepared. Then you will go back to bed satisfied and without the nagging worry and if you follow your physiological relaxation routine, you should soon be comfortably asleep again. You won't miss that half hour because you will sleep more deeply with an easy mind.

HELPING THE ILL PATIENT

This section is for physiotherapists and nurses, or for relatives looking after a member of their family. It is presumed the doctor in charge has given permission for this treatment to be used.

Sometimes I have been asked to help patients who were tense and unhappy but too ill from varying causes to apply their minds at that moment to understand the underlying reasons for their tension, and who therefore would have been unable to carry out the joint changes themselves with any accuracy. In one instance when I called at the home of a child patient I found him in the middle of an attack of asthma. Often, in hospital, I have been asked to help a woman at the end of the first stage of labour, who was in great distress, and had not learned any relaxation or helpful breathing antenatally. I once treated a most fragile patient in this way. She was a lady approaching her 102nd birthday and had developed a chest condition. She recovered well and could look forward to her birthday party in a few weeks.

METHOD

Do not disturb the patient in any way, but see that there are plenty of pillows near at hand, for support when the patient begins to relax. If he is leaning forward as he may well be, grasping his hands across his chest, leave him as he is and place enough pillows behind his back so that when he leans back later his head will be supported. Patients with breathing difficulties will always be found sitting up.

If the patient is lying down let him stay there; it is most important not to frighten the patient or try to reorganize him too soon. Do not appear brisk or hearty. Sit down quietly facing the patient so that your chair is about opposite his chest. Say in a quiet voice 'Perhaps I can help you to get more comfortable; let us try'. Do not say you are going to relax him, because that is probably the last thing he wants. He is frightened to lose the defensive tension.

You are going to undermine that tension so that it begins to disappear, and the patient will then begin to cooperate. You are going to handle the patient gently and fairly quickly into the ease positions. As you do so you gently say the orders. Do not expect to get full results in all joints at once. You will only get that in this case after repetition.

Place each hand gently over the top of the shoulders saying quietly 'Pull your shoulders towards your feet'. You gently press his shoulders downwards, then slip the palms of your hands around his arms saying 'Elbows out and open' and gently assist his arms away from his sides and the lower arms open at the elbows with his hands lying on his abdomen. The whole of both arms should remain supported on bed or pillows.

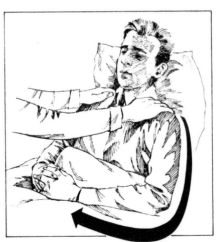

28 Helper handling patient's shoulders, elbows, and hands into ease positions

29 The resulting position

Continue moving your hands down towards his wrists saying 'Fingers long and supported' while you stretch his fingers and thumbs out gently so that they lie out flat. All this you do in one long continuous flowing movement of your two hands. Then repeat all from the beginning. Keep on talking as you handle the limbs into quietude adding 'Feel the comfortable position', then pausing slightly. The patient will now be getting a multitude of impulses to his brain registering the ease positions, and a certain amount of comfort from the touch of your hands, and he is probably assisting you in the movements.

Immediately proceed to the orders 'Press your body into the bed' (p. 90). Give a slight push with your hand flat on his breast bone. This is followed by 'Press your head into the pillow' (p. 91) and this should be assisted by your gentle pushing with your hand encircling his lower jaw or on his forehead. Place your finger tips in front on the angle between the ribs on the upper part of the abdomen above the waist, and say 'Breathe out gently and easily' and let the slight weight of your fingers press a little inwards as the breath comes out. Do not force or count, but follow the movement of the patient.

Then slip each hand in a curve around each side of the lower ribs and say 'When you are ready take an easy breath in and push my hands sideways'. As the patient achieves this say 'Breathe out when you are ready'. While he does so, gently press on the ribs making your hands follow a curve downwards and inwards, again following

30 Helper pressing
body into the bed

the movements of the patient's chest. Keep your hands where they
are, and ask the patient to breathe in again expanding all the way
round and to breathe out when he wishes. As he breathes in coax the
rib movement out and up with your hands and as he breathes out
give the slight pressure on the ribs as before.

If you think the patient would like to repeat the breathing, move
your finger tips to where they were previously and repeat the whole
performance as above. Never let the patient do more deep breathing than this at a time. Accentuate the outward breath, but do not
prolong it unduly, and be certain that the patient dictates the rate of
breathing—not you. You must respect his respiratory centre in his
brain and not annoy it. You are only trying to help him to use his
diaphragm muscle and to aerate the lower larger area of his lungs
more fully.

You might then go over the arms, hands, body, and head changes
again. You'll probably gain considerably more joint changes and
resulting relaxation.

If the patient has now closed his eyes, or in any way looks more
comfortable, begin on the face changes, saying them slowly and
touching his lower jaw, with a gentle hand, helping him to drag his
jaw down. Ask him to concentrate on feeling his loose lips and
separated teeth, and to make his tongue lie in the middle of his
mouth.

Then place a light finger tip of either hand at the corner of his eyes
and gently stretch sideways saying 'Close your eyes' and ask him to
enjoy the pleasant darkness. If he does not close his eyes, ignore it.
He will do so when he feels more comfortable.

31 Helper pressing head
into the pillow

Then place the palm of one hand gently on his forehead and say
'Smooth your forehead up, and continue over the top of your head
and down the back of your neck', sweeping your hand slowly over
his forehead and head as you talk. Possibly repeat twice—no more.
Patients always enjoy this, but only do this movement when the
patient is getting relaxed and so is ready to receive it. He may then
close his eyes.

Your whole attitude should be one of calm control. Do not use a
soporific or affected voice—just be natural and quiet. Handle the
patient fairly firmly though gently. It is calming to feel that the
person handling your limbs is in charge and can be trusted. Work
around the body much more quickly than with the ordinary person.
The essence is repetition and gradual encouragement of the patient
to work with you.

You add the hip, knee and feet changes when you have got the top
half of the patient some way into the ease positions, and you think
he is ready to accept them.

Do not disturb the bedclothes, just roll the legs apart and turned
outwards, with your hands on top of the bedclothes as you say 'Turn
your hips outwards'. You may need to give the feet rather a sustained push to get them to bend down at the ankles. The bedclothes
should be loosely over the feet at all times. Encourage the patient to
work with you by saying 'Push your feet away from your face'.

As you work with the patient you are of course observing him
very closely. Immediately you see real signs of ease in the patient—a
calmer face or a sigh is a good sign—say 'See if you can help me'.
You then repeat the order and the change you were already doing.
As you continue gently to handle the patient into position he will
start working with you.

Immediately this happens encourage the registration of feeling: 'Can you feel your elbows are away from your sides and open? Can you feel your finger tips touching the sheet? Can you feel your head is pushed into the pillow? Does that feel better?' Don't tell him—ask him. You aren't trying to bully him into relaxation, but assist him to find the way to do it for himself.

For this kind of patient the word 'comfortable' is more acceptable than 'relaxed'. They long to be comfortable but they daren't relax, so they must feel, by what you assist them to do, that these are the same thing. When the patient has realized by his obvious enjoyment of your treatment that to be comfortable is to be relaxed, you can use the word and then proceed when suitable to the whole routine as described in Chapter 4, if acceptable to the patient. On the first occasion, however, leave the patient alone as soon as comfort is achieved. Ten to fifteen minutes at the most should be spent and only as long as that if the patient is enjoying it. Sleep may be of primary importance.

Before you leave you suggest quietly that the patient may like to do for himself what you have been doing together. Then don't say goodbye, just disappear silently.

On other occasions when arranging pillows, etc., gently assist the patient into the ease positions, especially head supported by a pillow, arms out from the sides, and open at the elbows, possibly resting on other pillows and fingers long and supported. Try to see the legs are uncrossed and parted. They will always come together again. Never blame the patient for this or any other 'bad' position. Help him out of it saying 'This will be more comfortable for you'.

PEOPLE WITH BREATHING DIFFICULTIES

Anyone who has chest problems should of course consult his doctor. Possibly the patient will be sent for physiotherapy. His own particular needs will be assessed, and dealt with, and he will be taught how to manage his own chest as much as possible. Chemotherapy, various machines and nebulisers, are now frequently used in conjunction with chest physiotherapy, and should only be used by those specializing in the subject, or by those who have been taught by them.

What the patient can do for himself is to become really expert at positioning, relaxation and true diaphragmatic breathing plus any exercises, coughing, etc. he has already had selected for him and been taught. The patient may wish to teach a relative who could then aid him when in difficulties but it is important that the relative simply assists and never attempts to dictate. The patient must remain in charge of his own treatment.

On pp. 53-54 there is a brief description of normal diaphragmatic breathing. Let us now consider the complete mechanism of the chest.[3] This will, I think, give those who suffer from their chest, great confidence in the structures they are trying to get to work for their own benefit. I have so often treated patients struggling for breath, who had accumulated the most weird collection of ideas about breathing which made it impossible for them to use what facilities they had properly.

Some people teach odd variations of the normal breathing rhythm hoping thereby to induce relaxation. I am not in favour of this interference with normal physiology.

The chief muscle of breathing is the diaphragm.[4] This is a dome-shaped muscle with its curve upwards forming the floor of the chest and its contents, and the ceiling of the abdomen and its contents. It is like a mushroom whose stalk is firmly attached to the spine at the back and whose lower free edge is attached all around to the six lower ribs. It has two domes with a flattened area between where the heart lies. It is like a tent projecting so far upwards into the rib cage that the liver which it covers and which stretches from the right side across to the left nipple line, is contained under the ribs.[5] It is for this reason that when the diaphragm contracts the two domes, which move first, can only descend a limited amount as the diaphragm is then fixed by its own attachments and rests on the upper surface of the liver, which is also tethered in place by ligaments.[6] It does however, increase the pressure within the abdomen which is always greater than the atmosphere. Thus, if you place your fingers in the angle of the ribs in front, you feel slight bulging just between the right and left curve of the rib cage. Your fingers are of course resting on the front of your liver or part of your guts lying under your abdominal muscles.[7] This area is often erroneously described as 'the diaphragm', which is very muddling for people who are trying to understand its action. After all the ancient Jews knew the diaphragm lay above the liver. In Exodus it is frequently referred to as 'the caul above the liver'.

As your diaphragm continues to contract it moves its only remaining moveable area which is attached to the ribs and lifts them outwards and upwards with the muscles between the ribs (external intercostals) assisting. This performing two movements is a common habit of muscles e.g. the first movement of the biceps is to rotate the forearm so that the palm of the hand is uppermost (supination) and then to bend up the elbow.[8] The ribs move like the handle of a bucket being lifted up, as they have two specially shaped joints, one smooth one at the back where they meet the vertebrae and one in front. This latter junction is made of the softish kind of bone called cartilage where they meet the breast bone (sternum).

Each rib is bent, twisted and wider and longer than the one above it. The upper ribs are much more fixed than the lower ones. As the lower ribs swing out and up they increase the width of the chest. They eventually push forwards the lower part of the breast bone and so increase the dimension from front to back. The descent of about 2.5 cms. of the domes of the diaphragm of course increases the vertical dimension.[9]

Thus you create an increase in three dimensions in your chest. Because of this the pressure in the chest will be negative to the

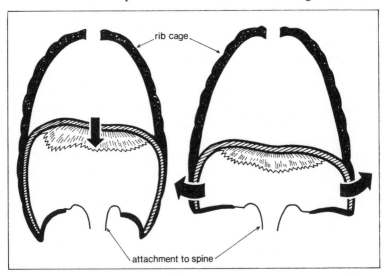

32 First movement: descent of the upper curve of the diaphragm onto liver

Second movement: showing attachment to ribs lifting them sideways and upwards

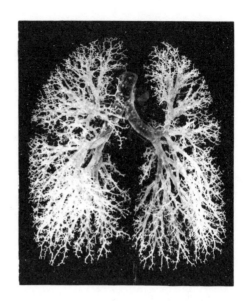

33 The lungs widen out lower down, as this photograph of the windpipe and its branches in the lung, makes clear. The rib cage also widens out to accommodate them. This is why you should breathe low in your chest.

positive outside pressure and air will immediately flow into the lungs to try to equalize it.

Interchange of carbon dioxide and oxygen then takes place between the blood stream and the air. When messages reach the breathing centre that the carbon dioxide content of the blood is lowered, and when the elastic lungs are stretched to a certain degree there is a signal to the breathing centre and messages come back from it to the working muscles, to relax. The diaphragm relaxes upwards under your lungs, pressing against them and helping to empty them. The ribs also fall downwards and inwards, pressing the lungs from all sides. Normal breathing out is entirely passive.

The breathing rhythm is then repeated at a signal from the breathing centre.

When a patient understands all this he is not content just to let his chest shunt up and down like a solid box as it desperately tries to take in air, instead of using its natural expansive capabilities. When for any reason he finds his breathing rhythm becoming upset he knows exactly what to do to relieve his distress.
This is:

1.   Adopt a chosen position that by experience he knows suits him.

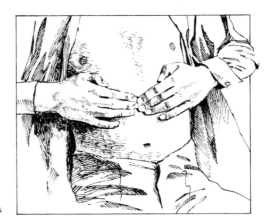

34 Patient's hands feeling
upper abdomen moving
forwards and ribs sideways

2.   Go through the physiological relaxation changes beginning with his own key change.

3.   Gain control of his diaphragm and low chest breathing.

He will of course be happier upright rather than lying and in a position that supports as much of his body as possible, sitting leaning either forwards or backwards.

The patient should already have learned physiological relaxation (Chapter 4). He should have practised the whole technique often when he is not breathless, so that when an attack occurs he can visualize the relaxed positions and use them as quickly and as fully as possible. He should begin with his key position (Chapter 5 p. 64) and as he is getting into position, try via the technique to reduce the use of the extra muscles that are working. Pull the shoulders down, elbows out and open, fingers long and supported on the lower part of his chest, with the finger tips resting in the little hollow at the lower end of the breast bone. At the same time he should try to push the head onto some suitable support. He should repeat all possible joint changes throughout the attack especially registering the ease positions. This often allays the spiral of terror that may overtake the patient. He should continue going over the changes as he deals with his diaphragm.

As the attack begins he should try immediately, while getting into his relaxed position, to retain or regain control of the lower chest breathing.[10] The breathing will tend to have become quicker and high in the chest and it is urgent that he should try to prevent this increasing.

He is going to try to breathe low down in his chest under his relaxed hands. He should *not* try to change the pace at first. He should breathe out as easily as he can, neither forcing nor prolonging it. Then as he breathes in, he feels the hollow under his finger tips bulge slightly forwards and his ribs expand sideways under his palms.

He should concentrate on this action and ignore the fact that he is still breathing too quickly, for this is the true diaphragmatic movement, and as he gains control of that, his distress will start to abate.

He continues at any pace dictated by necessity, keeping the breath out very easy and never lengthened unduly. Gradually he will feel his upper chest breathing slacken its desperation, and he can then gradually decrease the rate of his diaphragmatic breathing. He continues the joint changes for deeper relaxation. Breathing out should always be easy.

Place then *Pace* will give relief, as will performing the physiological technique at the beginning, throughout, and at the end of the attack of breathlessness. By resting his head and arms he helps to get relaxation in the neck muscles which insist on rushing into action whenever breathing is difficult. This prolongs the unproductive upper chest breathing where the chest and lungs are so much narrower. Increased muscle work of any kind increases the breathlessness, so obviously conscious relaxation of muscular activity will help to reduce it.

When he feels a little happier he should not hurry out of his comfortable position. He should stay and have some rest, relaxing all over and keeping breathing low down in his chest and easy till he feels really better.

ANTENATAL, LABOURING, AND POSTNATAL MOTHERS

The physiologist F. Halberg, who investigated the daily cycle of the body and invented the word circadian, has shown by statistics what practising midwives already knew, that the highest number of births take place about 4 a.m.[11] He points out that the mother's daily metabolic cycle is at its lowest at this hour, and

An antenatal mother practising physiological relaxation alone in her own home.

therefore she will probably be, naturally, in her most relaxed state. So we appear to be fitting in with nature's dictates, which are usually wise, when we teach antenatal mothers a technique of relaxation that has proved workable.

Antenatal preparation courses have been based on relaxation since pioneers Miss Minnie Randall and Dr Grantly Dick-Read about the nineteen twenties first suggested its importance, and since then midwives have seen and appreciated the results in their patients. I myself have been teaching antenatal mothers relaxation since 1935.

It is a good idea for the antenatal mother to attend training classes, preferably in a small group in the hospital where the birth is to take place, so as to become familiar with the place and the staff and their usual procedures. If the birth is to take place at home, she should join a class whose teacher is in touch with the methods of her prospective team. In either case she should ask all the questions she wants and air all her difficulties. I have already made a cassette tape for teaching physiological relaxation and other training for antenatal mothers and applying it to labour. It is much used by physiotherapists and midwives in this and other countries, so I shall just give a few guidelines here.

The pregnant woman learns physiological relaxation for the following reasons:

1.   To help her during pregnancy when she may have special physical difficulties, to relieve tension and induce real rest.

2.   To develop *deep* relaxation to use *during* contractions in the first stage of labour, and extremely *quick* relaxation control for use *between* contractions in the second stage.

3.   After the baby is born to deal with tensions, physical (e.g. feeding the baby) and emotional, and to encourage a lifetime habit of tension control.

PREGNANCY

It is important that a pregnant woman rests on her bed every day for an hour.[12] She will decide the exact time for herself, usually after lunch or before supper, depending on her commitments. Physiological relaxation is invaluable for helping to obtain complete rest and to release tension if she has times of fear or panic, which is common and not at all surprising. In fact, having a baby is a very emotional time for both parents. Prospective fathers find physiological relaxation easy to learn. They are usually taught it by their wives. It is useful to know so that they can help their wives as well as themselves. It is a great comfort to a pregnant woman to know that fear of delivery, and other worries are usual symptoms though varying in degree, and to find a technique that she can use at any time by herself alone, that will help her to deal with them. By attending training classes, too, she will find much comfort in the knowledge and understanding gained and in discussing her feelings with others.

Circulation   Total rest for an hour daily with the feet up helps the circulation around the body. The mother needs this because of the increased amount of blood she makes during pregnancy.[13] Repeated pushing down of the feet at the ankle when performing physiological relaxation helps the circulation up from the legs. This action should be done carefully and slowly as some women get muscle cramp easily.

If at any time, e.g. during the night, cramp develops, she should use the reciprocal relaxation technique and tell the opposite group of muscles to work. If the cramp is in the back of the lower leg—as it frequently is—she should try to lie quietly and tell the foot to bend upwards at the ankle and thus get relaxation messages to the muscles working at the back. She should not force with the hands or rub the leg or foot. This often makes it worse. She should just go on telling her foot to bend upwards. When enough messages have passed down to the lower leg she will find the cramp will suddenly let go and her foot will bend up. The pain at the back of the leg and in the foot immediately disappears. I have proved this for myself many times. Eventually you learn to bend your feet upwards just as the cramp begins and so you can often prevent it.

Positions for relaxing   Positions for learning are as described in Chapter 4, p. 44. Some pregnant women, however, may not be comfortable lying on their backs at the beginning, because they cannot relax. When they have learned the technique, they often prefer this position. Anyone who still does not like it, should try lying on her side, with a pillow pulled down almost parallel with the body so that it receives the top arm, the chest, and the head. The underarm goes behind, or she may prefer to put it

35, 36 Starting positions
for pregnant women

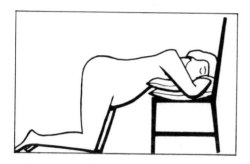

under the head pillow and the under leg is almost straight while the top leg is bent at the hip and knee and supported on another pillow.

She must always get down onto hands and knees, then put the head on the pillow and so roll over onto her back. She must also roll over onto hands and knees to get up. She may damage her already stretched tummy muscles, if she just sits and then lowers herself backwards. When lying flat in bed, on floor or examination couch, she should not just heave herself up head first, or again she may damage her tummy muscles or her back, as the strain is so great. She should roll over onto hands and knees or swing her legs over the edge of the bed, and then push herself up with her hands to sitting, using her strong back muscles and not vulnerable tummy ones.

Alternatives to lying down are the 2 sitting positions, with head and arm support or kneeling, as in the picture above. Gentle pelvic tilting is often comforting. Do not remain too long in this position or you may strain your back.

Any of these is often very comfortable in the later months,

although I have known many women who liked relaxing on their backs right up to term. Of course if any woman feels sick or faint in any position she must change at once. In any case antenatal mothers and indeed everyone should be encouraged to change position when practising physiological relaxation. They should try different positions, and also change from one to another during any session. It gave me great pleasure during a class for antenatal mothers to see them roll over from one position to another. Perhaps one would stand up and go over and get herself comfortable and relaxed again, sitting at a table while I was talking. I knew, then, they really were appreciating the sensations of their own bodies and could attend to their own needs. Relaxation is not some precious attribute to be hoarded and treated with awe. One should be able to use it or discard it, or use it in another context, as easily as a woman changes her mind.

In the later months, in fact sometimes earlier, it is often difficult to get comfortable in bed, and the ability to relax in different positions is often a help, as change is essential to relieve strained muscles. The side lying position with the top leg resting on a pillow may soothe the strain.

Relaxation technique   This is basically exactly the same as in Chapter 4 and the mothers should first learn the technique exactly as set out there. They should then experience this in varying positions which they may want to adopt as pregnancy advances. Then they should practice timing of relaxation—very deep and concentrated for the first stage of labour, and extremely swift for the second stage.

They may wish to associate relaxation with breathing changes and also changes of position. The main point is that the mothers should feel they have mastered a technique which they will use themselves for their own comfort as and when they want to. They should also practise while disturbing noise is produced around them. When I held antenatal training classes, visitors often attended to watch. We made use of them by asking them to walk about while the mothers practised the relaxation technique as I called out the changes. Then they were asked to stand beside the relaxed mothers and talk to and look at them and discuss their positions and even to touch them. The mothers loved it and were very proud of their ability to ignore all this bombardment and still relax. Of course if any girl appeared to be disturbed in any way by these attentions I removed the watchers at once, until she had developed more relaxation control.

This was wonderful training for the eventual delivery when there would be some disturbance and strangers watching in a difficult situation.

LABOUR

During the final weeks a woman is often conscious of a hard feeling across her abdomen. This is a forerunner of the labour contractions. It is a great help to her, if instead of trying to ignore this, she gives it her attention and so begins to register what *the result* of a muscular wave of contraction is like that is completely outside her control. As she feels this, she should practise her relaxation technique in so far as this is practical. This depends on where she happens to be at the time. She is then training herself, before she is in actual labour, in exactly what she is going to do when labour is established.

When labour is established the old fashioned idea was 'to keep busy'. Ironing was much favoured, and some women even turned out cupboards—'nest building' it was sometimes called. This was all really a way of trying to use up the tension of the old fear reflex. But surely, we have a better way. This woman is going to perform in the second stage the hardest work she will ever do. It must be wise for her to rest during the first stage as much as possible—all athletes rest before exertion.

Don't let us have any woman in first stage of labour careering madly around cleaning her home, wearing out her energy in response to a primitive reflex. Let her guard her strength. So before labour she practises deep relaxation for use in the first stage preferably against a disturbing background, and an instantaneous relaxation after effort for the second stage.

Tell the Team It is wise for the mother to say, at the start, to the team looking after her that she has been practising a relaxation technique which she hopes to use during labour. They will probably be aware of this and will certainly welcome it. If the husband is hoping to attend the delivery this will also have been discussed with the staff. He should be aware of the probable course of labour, the techniques his wife has learned, and how he can assist her as she uses these during each stage. He will probably have attended classes.

First Stage At each contraction she should select a position from those she has already learned in training class or from pp. 44 and 100. She begins her relaxation changes with an easy outward breath from low in her chest. She breathes in easily there and continues thus as she goes through—with deep concentration—all the changes of physiological relaxation. This she has already practised and so, as the contraction builds up until it is finally at its height, there she is resting, relaxed and in control. She then stays as she is until the contraction has passed off, checking on all her joints to be sure they are still in the ease positions.

Between contractions she may wish to continue to rest or perhaps sometimes to walk around, make the odd cup of coffee, etc., but all in an easy manner ready to welcome and respond to each contraction with

1. Positioning
2. Physiological Relaxation
3. Breathing low in the chest.

What she is later going to do, the hard work of delivering a new human being, is much too important to have any energy that may be needed for that, dissipated in frantic useless activity.

Late First Stage This is of unknown duration. It is the final stretching of the outlet of the womb (dilatation of the cervix). When this is complete the second stage has begun and the mother can push if she and the midwife want her to. Often, however, the mother has an urge to push before final dilatation is complete. Of course pushing would not help the baby through an opening that was not yet large enough for him to pass through. The contractions are also now probably rather strong and close together although, of course, this varies. Every delivery is a unique performance.

The answer to all this is to try to maintain total relaxation during and between all contractions. The mother will then be as fresh as possible for the big moment when she is told she is fully dilated. She knows then she has completed the most frustrating part and now the real hard work begins. Delivery, we hope, is near and she can look forward to her baby in her arms very soon.

Second Stage In the second stage the mother may be asked by her team of helpers to remain relaxed and allow the uterus to do its own work without any extra assistance from her, or she may be encouraged to push if she wishes. She will, of course, be timing this very carefully with the pushing movement which is already taking place in her uterus, so that her maximum push, downwards and forwards, coincides with the maximum contraction of the uterus. After this moment, as she knows, the contraction starts to fade away, just as in the first stage. This is when she should immediately begin her relaxation changes in all her joints, and of course, as she has practised this, she can do it in seconds. She is able to use, for comfort, not only the time during the fading of the contraction, but also the time between the contractions, though this may be as little as half a minute. Thus she is better able to fit in with the cycle of maximum activity and maximum rest which appears to be nature's intention for an efficient, quick and safe emptying of the uterus.

It may be, as she has been warned at her antenatal training classes, that the cycle of performance of her uterus will be quite different from this. It will certainly be an individual performance, as every birth of every mother is always different from every other. Her job will then be to fit in with the directions of the team who are helping her, and if she is not pushing consciously to be consciously in a relaxed state. She should remember to begin to change to the ease positioning the instant the contraction *starts* to lessen.

The position adopted by the mother in the second stage may vary from squatting, sitting, walking about, to side lying or half sitting up supported by pillows behind her back, on the bed. In any position, if she is pushing, she will find it easier with her head forward, chin in, and legs bent. She may be supported by her husband or another member of the team. Immediately the contraction begins to pass off, she should seek support for her head, legs and body.

She will find the arm and hand changes of particular help in whatever position she may find herself—shoulders down, elbows out, fingers long and separated in one long quick stream of relaxation. She simply flicks out her fingers and thumbs into a stretched and open position and when she lets go, the pads of the fingers and thumbs are on some support. She may find she clenches her hands somewhat when she is pushing downwards and forwards; this does not matter so long as she undoes this immediately the contraction is passing off. She should not grasp her husband's hand for comfort, but let him hold her wrist, or let him put his hand over hers as he says

'Long and supported'. She flashes the other changes over the rest of her body. By practice, using her key position (p. 64), all this can happen almost simultaneously. So she gets some rest, even for a moment or two, until the next contraction begins.

Third Stage   The technique varies with different teams and each individual delivery. The mother's job is to follow any directions or if not actually assisting, to relax all over her body using the usual orders.

POSTNATAL PERIOD

The mother will of course be given daily exercises to regain her figure and especially to strengthen those internal pelvic muscles that support the womb and vaginal passage and that were stretched when the baby was born. She should never perform any exercise involving two leg lifting, or lifting forward her top half with her toes under a heavy piece of furniture. She can do great harm to those muscles and to her abdominal muscles and can also injure her spine.

She will be asked to rest for some time in the day, possibly on her face. During these times she should relax fully and even go to sleep. Postnatal mothers are very busy. They need rest.

I do hope all mothers will carry on the habit of trying to rest sometime during the day, fully relaxed, for at least half an hour. They should try to choose a time when the baby is also asleep and just skip the housework for a while. This daily habit of rest often prevents various troubles later on, and ensures they are ready, when their husbands return from work, to welcome them.

OSTEO-ARTHRITIS OF THE NECK AND SPINAL COLUMN

Please remember osteo-arthritis is a local condition of joint changes due to 'wear and tear'. It is totally different from rheumatoid arthritis, which is an illness affecting the whole patient and requires different treatment.

It was during an acute attack of this horrid complaint, osteo-arthritis, that I discovered this method of relaxation (p. 15) and I want to say a little more about its use when wearing a supporting collar which is often ordered as treatment. Physiological relaxation is now part of the routine treatment in some orthopaedic hospitals for osteo-arthritis and knowing how it helped me, I am glad for the sake of the patients.

Because the joints of the patient's neck are unstable and because, due to their loss of joint space as will have been shown in X-ray, the bones may press on some nerve roots which lie near the spinal column, the patient is in some degree of pain. He is also in fear of greater pain as he has probably experienced this on other occasions. All this makes the patient unconsciously tighten the neck muscles to try to fix his slipping joints and so carry the weight of his heavy head (about 5 kilos) without undue pressure on joints or nerves and resulting pain. It is to relieve this state that a supporting collar is worn.

There are many different kinds of support but they have one aim in common—to transfer the weight of the head to the bones of the shoulder girdles (i.e. collar bone and shoulder blade) and so relieve the strain on the seven distorted neck joints. The relief when this collar is first applied is tremendous. One feels as though a great pressing weight has been removed—which indeed it has.

The temptation, then, is to rest one's chin gratefully on the support and *sag*. Oh, the pleasure of being able to let go and know your head will be held up for you. Often you will see someone walking about the streets in this position—huddled into the collar which grips around the back of the neck and supports the lower jaw, his eyes are fixed forwards and he never so much as turns his head an inch to either side. You will see him swivel his eyes around to see things—his head remaining rigid. You can tell that under that collar every neck muscle is becoming weaker and weaker. How is he ever going to be able, therefore, to carry the weight of his own head again when the acute stage of his arthritis has passed?

I had to wear a collar for months on end and thereafter off and on for years, but now never need one except perhaps when motoring over very rough ground. I have also fitted many on other people and trained them in their use and how to strengthen their neck muscles so that they can do without the collar. These are my suggestions based on this experience, if this treatment is permitted by the doctor in charge:

Practise physiological relaxation (Chapter 4). This takes care of the resulting tensions caused by the very real and correct fear associated with pain.

Start to re-educate the neck muscles while still wearing your collar. They can then resume their task of head holding and control as soon as possible.

Begin with the three point pull (p. 82) then move your head very gently in any direction that you like. Stop immediately you begin to feel the slightest pain. Repeat the three point pull, and move the head in exactly the opposite direction. Repeat all this as your confidence grows and as you probably gain slightly more movement. Move cautiously. Stop immediately you feel the slightest twinge of the sharp pain down the arm or up into the head caused by pressure on the nerve root at the joint. You will learn to differentiate between this and the discomfort of stretching stiff muscles to their correct length. This stretching will be helpful to you and should be carefully encouraged.

Your movements are of course limited by the collar and the collar in fact gives resistance to some movements. Any time you get even a flicker of nerve root pain you immediately *stop* and do the physiological joint changes of your head and arms. You then return to exercise when you feel ready to do so but never for more than one minute at a time. So you give yourself alternate sessions of (a) complete rest on collar, (b) activity, and stretching, (c) physiological relaxation.

Some people have to wear the collar in bed, and others substitute it for a small hard pillow pulled well in to support the neck. When in bed, whether in collar, or on pillow, continue the regime of physiological relaxation, total rest interspersed with occasional one minute hard pressing against the support in all directions possible. The one thing you must not do is lift your head forwards off the pillow. This is much too great a strain for the damaged joints. Roll over and get up using the muscles at the back of your head to take the weight. You can also support your head with your hands.

You will probably be amazed how far you can 'pull your shoulders towards your feet' with your head lying motionless on the pillow. This will show you the amount of tension and probable shortening you can get in the large muscles which have been trying to help the smaller deep neck muscles to hold up your heavy head, poised as it is on the seven neck joints.

Meantime, you have three objectives to attain that will help you to do without the comforting collar, and be free again. For of course after the first relief from pain, and delight in the support, one really does feel in a prison and one longs for freedom.

1. Train yourself in physiological relaxation so that you have a weapon against pain and the tensions causing further deformity.

2. Strengthen the small muscles by repeated short doses of movement of the head in every direction, as previously described, while supporting the weight of the head on collar or pillow.

3. Relax and stretch the big muscles (trapezius etc.) by the three point pull. These have become shortened and possibly thickened.

These supporting muscles have been on continual duty due to the tension caused by pain. They are very tired, and heavy with fatigue products (p. 38). Therefore gentle massage and some infra-red heat treatment may be ordered to relieve this condition. But the main responsibility for recovery I believe, is on the patient, not on passive treatment, however pleasant. This should just be an intermittent treat, not continued for too long.

The same sort of regime as that described above I have found to be useful for myself and other patients with osteo-arthritis of other joints of the spine. The spine may be supported in a corset or by being in bed. Again, practise physiological relaxation to relieve the muscular tensions caused by pain. So do not do any bending forward or leg forward lifting, but perform all other movements of the spine and pelvis gently within the limit of pain, gradually trying to extend the possibilities: pelvic rocking, side bending, twisting around and bending backwards can be performed in bed lying either on the back or side.

Especially strengthen the back muscles, by pressing head, elbows, and heels into the bed to make 'Five holes in the Bed' for one minute. Do not just arch the back as you do this. You are trying to strengthen the muscles, not annoy the arthritic joints. Work against the resistance of the mattress as you press backwards making five *holes*. Work very hard, hold the final position for one minute, then

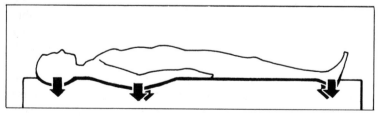

37 'Five holes in the bed'

slacken off. Do not hold the breath—singing or counting will stop this. Repeat once only. Perform morning and evening in bed lying flat on your back.

The regime therefore is the same as for arthritis of the neck. Rest, physiological relaxation and muscle training without causing any root pressure pain, should lead you to freedom and normal activity.

Deal With It   One often hears someone say with a self-pitying sigh 'Ah well, I've got osteo-arthritis, I've been told I must just learn to live with it'. May I suggest that by substituting the word 'deal' for 'live' we arthritics will get on much more agreeably. Let's be active in dealing with our osteo-arthritis. Don't just give in. Although the worn joints may remain rather unusual in shape it does not necessarily follow that pain, muscle weakness and inaction must continue. Let us deal with it, and learn how to get over the difficulties, so that we can continue to be of some use in the world instead of bundles of misery.

PSYCHIATRIC TREATMENT

Statistics from the National Association for Mental Health show that in 1974, 45% of all beds in National Health hospitals in England were occupied by mentally disturbed patients. They also tell us that one woman in every six, and one man in every nine, will probably enter hospital because of mental illness at least once during their lifetime. These figures are certainly arresting and while I don't for a moment see the method outlined here as a cure-all, it appears to have a part to play in the total area of psychiatric care.

I have no experience of treating psychiatric patients in groups, although I have treated many stressed patients, and so I am most grateful to Dr W. H. Newnham, consultant psychiatrist responsible for rehabilitation, and Mrs Jean Abbott, Superintendent Physiotherapist, of the Towers Hospital, Leicester, England, for their invitation to spend three days at their hospital. For some years they have used the physiological method of relaxation in treating their patients with satisfactory results, and I was able to join in many groups and discussions by both staff and patients, and actually experience this for myself. There are of course various other hospitals and clinics using this method where I have been kindly invited to visit. It seemed wise however to describe only one hospital routine as an example.

The following appears to be their accepted programme. The patients are treated in groups—never called classes—of men and women. About an hour is spent, partly in physiological relaxation and partly in discussion. The patients lie on the floor on mats with one pillow under the head and the only change in their usual clothing is that they remove their shoes. The arrangement on the floor is quite irregular, everyone choosing where they prefer to lie. The physiotherapist in charge of the group sits throughout in a chair. The atmosphere is easy and friendly and the patients seem to have no difficulty in voicing their own ideas and experiences.

Each group of course varies in its composition and arrangement, according to the clinical status and therapeutic needs of the patients. Here is an example of a group which I personally observed.

First of all the physiotherapist called out the orders for changes in all joints, then when the patients seemed properly relaxed they were asked to think for a few minutes of the happiest occasion they could remember that had happened in their experience. After a pause they were asked to think of the most unpleasant thing that had happened to them in the last week; meantime they tried to retain their ease positions.

The group then discussed, still lying on the floor, with great frankness, what unfortunate experiences had happened to them and also what part of their relaxation they had found easy to sustain, and what parts difficult. The physiotherapist, who of course is very skilled in this work, showed great judgment in her comments to each patient. Then they had another session of relaxation followed by further discussion of particular needs of individual patients. This is not a routine that should be conducted by an amateur or even a physiotherapist unversed in psychological medicine. The physiotherapy staff of the Towers Hospital are immersed in the dynamic psychiatric environment and are regarded as agents of the psychotherapeutic process.

In the out-patients' group, physiological relaxation and discussion are also intermingled. The patients were sometimes asked what nervous habits or positions they had noticed in other people during the previous week. These were discussed seriously by the group, yet with some enjoyment and laughter. Later they were asked what habits of tension they had noticed in themselves and what joint changes they had found helpful to overcome these. This led to another group discussion.

The patients seemed to have developed a good understanding of the relationship between unpleasant emotions and body tensions. They were quite articulate in describing exactly how their own bodies reacted and displayed satisfaction at their own control, and honesty about any difficulty. They were at the same time gaining an insight into mind-body relationships. They had been able to use the method on their own increasingly and some were being discharged as being in no need of further treatment. It was noticeable how self confident these patients seemed to be in expectation of being able to control their own tensions in the future.

The number of relaxation sessions given to patients varied from once weekly upwards as seemed necessary. Patients were encouraged to continue to use the relaxation technique by themselves in their daily life.

An important feature of the structure of therapy at the Towers Hospital is the weekly inter-disciplinary Staff meeting. At this meeting psychiatrists, occupational therapists, physiotherapists, nurses, social workers and so on, all of one team, fully discuss patients under their care. Thus all disciplines are made aware of the therapeutic assets within each patient, the treatment objectives and the attendant difficulties. No individual therapist is isolated and no therapist is left in an exposed position. Team morale is thus greatly strengthened.

7   Other methods

There is a welter of techniques at the moment suggested both by amateurs and those with professional experience to try to help people to cope with modern stress. Of these, three are notable: transcendental meditation, biofeedback and disassociation. So let us consider each briefly in the present context.

TRANSCENDENTAL MEDITATION AND RELAXATION RESPONSE

Herbert Benson of the Harvard Medical School has recently published a book about his work stemming from the problem of hypertension or high blood pressure.[1] It was noticed that hypertension was alleviated among people who were practising the Transcendental Meditation technique as developed by the Maharishi Mahesh Yogi.

Benson argues that the 'fight or flight' response which gives rise to hypertension, can be counteracted by the 'relaxation response' which is initiated by devoting short periods each day to meditation. He has evolved a simple set of instructions for meditation, for which he claims 'no innovation but simply a scientific validation of age-old wisdom'. He also points out that the Yogic technique is far from being the only one and much of its method is shared by other mystical or meditative traditions, like Zen, Sufism and indeed the tradition of Christian mysticism.

The instructions evolved by Benson and his team are to sit quietly and comfortably with closed eyes and a relaxed body and then to concentrate on a single word or phrase to the exclusion of other thoughts. Throughout a passive, take it or leave it attitude to the proceedings is essential.[2]

Some people who practise meditation have already told me that they use physiological relaxation to prepare for meditation. This seems a good idea, rather than just hoping relaxation will happen.

The limitation of any form of meditation is that it cannot be brought into play at those moments during the day when the fight or flight response actually makes itself felt in our bodies. It requires quiet, solitude, ten or fifteen minutes, and total disengagement of the mind from the process of ordinary thought and existence. Physiological relaxation, on the other hand, is quick, can be used in whole or in part, and be incorporated into one's active living—at one's desk, round the conference table, on the phone, in the car, at the sink. It is not to be viewed *instead of* meditation in whatever form but as a valuable skill *in addition* to it. Dr Benson calls relaxation response an 'innate body mechanism'. So too is the reciprocal relaxation of muscles. Let them therefore work side by side.

BIOFEEDBACK

The use of a biofeedback machine, it is claimed, makes it possible for the person using it to control his autonomic system (p. 121) and therefore, the glands and involuntary muscle controlled by this. Because involuntary muscle interlines the coats of blood vessels, blood pressure in some cases, can be controlled in this way.

Normally the autonomic system is entirely independent of one's will, but it is suggested that if the information from biofeedback can be brought to the upper consciousness, then the paths between the lower and upper parts of the brain can be retrained at will.

The biofeedback instruments vary from quite efficient home-made varieties to very expensive gadgets for indiscriminate sale. Some have been used as 'lie detectors'. They do not measure muscular tension but monitor the dampness of the skin as the person holds one lead in his hand. This information causes the movement of a needle on a dial and sometimes a high pitched noise varying in intensity as the needle rises. This is called the 'arousal state' since it is believed that sweating palms accompany other stress symptoms.

The idea is that the person using the machine takes this as a warning that the sympathetic system, i.e. the fight or flight system is going into action. He should then change his thoughts to a peaceful level and use the needle on the machine or the intensity of the noise to measure his resulting success.

If this technique is sufficiently understood by the person involved, and if he really uses the machine to understand what is happening, and if he really does retrain the results of his own biological feedback, which is going on all the time, then the instrument can be of use. But this is rather a lot of 'ifs'.

If, however, he merely becomes dependent on the machine, he is no further on the way to freedom from tension. Why not use the body's own internal biofeedback? You can learn via your own sensory system when your joints are in tense positions and break the vicious circle by performing physiological relaxation changes. The joints and skin surfaces will then 'feed back' a mass of beneficial messages to the brain both at the conscious level and below it.

The automatic result of this is immediate adjustment by the autonomic system to deal with the changed circumstances.

Thus we are using the interplay of the efficient body apparatus in a natural manner, while at the same time gaining greater control of it by understanding and practice within the boundaries of its own laws.

DISASSOCIATION

Disassociation—although I cannot find the word defined as such in any dictionary—is the name given by some people to a technique whereby one part of the body is consciously relaxed while another area is consciously tensed. I prefer to call it selective tension and relaxation.

Every dancer and every serious athlete is trained to do this. Some musicians are lucky enough to be taught to do so, and all need it. But, of course, one must first learn how to relax.

If we are not trained in control we tend to imagine that the more muscle tensions all over our body we produce the better we are working. This is not true. Unnecessary tensions simply weary us. We are all apt to tense many more muscles than is necessary for any task we are performing, whether it is playing a violin or chopping wood. When we speak of a 'graceful performer' we usually mean one whose muscles are working perfectly in harmony with no extra groups in action. On the other hand if you watch a very young child who is drawing a picture, you may notice the hunched up little shoulders, the screwed up face, and possibly the tongue wagging away, making the same movements as the crayon, as though in encouragement.

We all do this kind of thing, to a greater or lesser degree. For many people the learning of the skill of physiological relaxation will be quite enough for them to master their own extra tensions during normal daily activities. But you may care to practise tensions opposed to relaxation.

A few people use so-called 'disassociation' to help prepare antenatal mothers for the great dominating contraction of the uterus in labour and delivery. This does not seem a valid preparation, since the uterine contractions are not controlled from the conscious brain, and it may be very disconcerting to be overwhelmed by a contraction you cannot control when you have only practised those you can control (e.g. arm and leg), even if associated with relaxation elsewhere.

More and more obstetrical units, it seems, use physiological relaxation, as this trains conscious recognition of the relaxed positions. This is what the antenatal mother needs—conscious control of relaxation, not the creation of tensions, as any midwife will tell you. Application of the physiological relaxation method to antenatal, labouring, and postnatal mothers is explained on pp. 97-106.

In 1963 when I first made a gramophone record of the Mitchell method of physiological relaxation, I taught it on one side, and tension opposed to relaxation on the other. This was found useful by some people and I repeat it now, but in a slightly different form. So if you do want to play games with muscle actions here are a few suggestions—and a few warnings.

FIRST COMBINATION: ARMS

When you are lying or sitting, having completely relaxed your whole body by giving it the correct orders to change every joint position (see Chapter 4), concentrate on your hands.

Decide which hand you want to become active and which will remain relaxed. Then, keeping the relaxed hand and arm exactly as they are, consciously tense the fingers and thumb of the other hand into a punch; retain this punch, bend up the elbow; retain both the punch and the bent elbow, and bring the arm across the chest.

Now squeeze the punching hand, the bending elbow, and the flexed arm so that you intensify each position. Then press the whole arm hard against your chest. Continue the tension of the working arm, while feeling what the other arm and hand are doing, and check on the relaxed positions there. Are these still perfect? Proba-

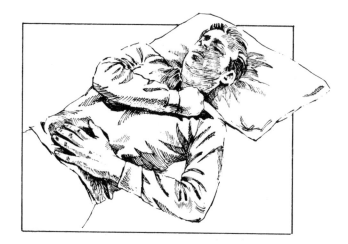

38 Selective
relaxation: right
arm tensed,
left arm relaxed

bly not, but don't worry. Put the working arm again into its starting position of complete relaxation and perhaps try again later if you wish.

SECOND COMBINATION: ARMS

Perform the actions as in the first combination and between each contraction of the working hand and arm, feel the identical joint of the other hand and arm. Feel if its position has altered at all in sympathy with the working arm. If it has, make it resume its ease position again. At the same time increase the tension at the working joint on the opposite arm.

In this way you will have a tense position in one joint and the ease position in the corresponding joint of the other arm, both being monitored by your own discriminating feeling at the same moment.

FIRST COMBINATION: LEGS

Lie on the floor then choose which leg will be active and which relaxed. Work one leg into the tense positions while keeping the other leg in the ease positions.

This is how you do it.

Bend one ankle stiffly upwards and make sure the other has the foot dangling loosely downwards. Now, keeping the foot stiffly upwards, bend the working knee and hip slightly by dragging the heel along the ground towards the buttock. Then make the thigh cross over the relaxed thigh slightly and press it there with heel still touching the floor. So now the working leg has a bent up foot, a bent knee, and hip, the thigh crossing over the other leg and tensing hard in all these positions. Check all the ease positions of the joints of the other leg. Now stop working so hard, uncross your working leg and just slide the heel along the floor to the position in which it started, lying beside the heel of the relaxed leg. Both legs are now lying straight on the ground.

SECOND COMBINATION: LEGS

Repeat the above combination but test your breathing and ensure all ease positions throughout the body. Feel the exact ease positions of your other joints in your accustomed way, altering them if necessary. Do this checking as you proceed with the activity of the working leg. At the zenith of the contraction of the working leg make a final check on all other joints, face, and breathing. Then return the working leg to its original position, as before, by sliding the heel along the floor away from the buttock.

When you can achieve all this fairly satisfactorily, choose for yourself what action you will give the working arm or leg to do.

39 Selective relaxation: right leg tensed, left leg relaxed

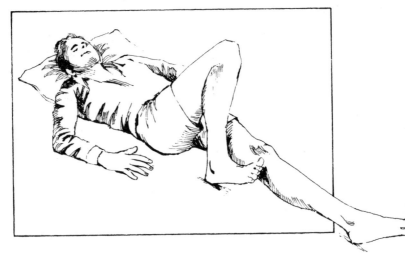

COMBINATIONS OF YOUR OWN COMPOSITION

Improvise your own combinations for different parts of your body to tense and move in any way you choose while remaining in the ease positions everywhere else. Each time when you reach the zenith of what is called 'the control'—the extreme tensing of the final position—test the relaxation not only of your other arm or leg but of the whole of your body, including breathing. If you know all the orders and positions and feelings of physiological relaxation well by your usual daily practise, this is a good test of your real ability. Were you holding your breath? Or you may have found that you had set your jaw, or tensed some other part to help your concentration.Of course, it doesn't really help your concentration. It is just a bad habit. Habits sometimes need to be recognized—and if necessary changed (Chapter 5).

Suggestions

1. *Lying*   Screw up your face, especially eyes and lips, and clench your jaw. At the same time stiffen up your feet into the tense position towards your face while concentrating on complete relaxation of arms, hands, body and head and easy breathing.

2. *Sitting*   Lift alternate knees towards your face so that alternate feet are just raised above the floor while maintaining relaxation in arms, head and body. The breathing may quicken because of the increased exercise. Allow this to happen but try to keep it low in your chest.

3. *Lying or sitting*   Clasp your hands together in front against your chest with the elbows bent, drag your jaw down but open your eyes wide and concentrate on looking at something. Meantime do the relaxation changes in your hips, knees, feet, body and head. Be aware of your breathing and if necessary correct it as usual.

4. *Sitting or standing*   Do some activity you have to perform daily, e.g. stirring a pan, typing, holding a steering wheel, hammering, etc. and maintain ease positions in all the other joints of the body not in use.

WARNING

Do not be tempted to lift both legs straight off the floor in any work-out. This can be most dangerous to the low back, abdominal muscles and pelvic floor, especially in women after childbirth. I have often had to treat both men and women who had sustained muscular, and in some cases bone damage by doing this. It is only safe for very active, very young men and women used to running up and down mountains—and they don't need it.

Please don't be persuaded to try it by someone who may tell you it will strengthen your tummy muscles. They probably do not realize the harm it can do. Certainly the abdominal muscles do try to work to assist in the great strain of trying to lift up those heavy long legs at a disadvantageous leverage.[3] But they are forced to work statically in a stretched position which is a great strain on them (see p. 38). This makes you hold your breath and the force all goes in your low back and the inside pelvic muscles which in women hold the womb and vagina in place. Damage may result and it tires the tummy muscles, instead of strengthening them so that they bulge out in front, and often become even more stretched. *Beware. Don't do it.*

Don't get annoyed with yourself if you find the combinations of tension and relaxation difficult. Don't despair and above all don't go on practising too long at one time. You are trying to gain control of your body—not punish it. If you don't really like this technique don't inflict it on yourself. You may be one of the people who do better practising physiological relaxation in daily living and can't be bothered playing games of tension and relaxation artificially combined. That's perfectly all right. Use your skill and practise it in the way that suits you best and gives you best results, in your own particular circumstances whatever your age.[4]

If you want to practise these games, only do so for a short time, and then forget about it. You can try again later. Little and often is the best plan. Remember the body learns by repetition.

If you try different combinations each time you will learn more about your mind and body associations.

Let us not be thwarted by the bad habit of uncontrolled muscle tension from enjoying our lives and continuing to develop fresh interests and new contacts with other people as long as we live.

REFERENCES

CHAPTER 1

1. D.H.S.S.
2. Registrar General for England and Wales.
3. Guyton, A. C., *Function of the Human Body,* Saunders, 4th edition 1974, p. 95.
4. Bourne G., *Pregnancy,* Cassell, 1972, pp. 340, 348, 350, 354.

CHAPTER 2

1. O'Connell A. and Gardner E., *Understanding the Scientific Bases of Human Movement,* Williams and Wilkins, 1972, p. 163
2. Basmajian J. V., *Primary Anatomy,* Williams and Watkins, 5th edition 1967, pp. 168, 169; Wells K. F., *Kinesiology,* Saunders, 5th edition 1971, pp. 161, 162.
3. Gardner W. D. and Osburn W. A., *Structure of the Human Body,* Saunders, 2nd edition 1973, p. 159.
4. Guyton A. C., *Structure and Function of the Nervous System,* Saunders, 1972, pp. 68, 69, 72, 76, 77, 81.
5. *Understanding the Scientific Bases of Human Movement,* pp. 179, 180; Lewis p. and Rubenstein D., *The Human Body,* Hamlyn, 1973, pp. 130, 131.
6. *Understanding the Scientific Bases of Human Movement,* pp. 209, 211.
7. ibid., pp. 194-197; *Function of the Human Body,* p. 312; *Structure and Function of the Nervous System,* p. 159.
8. Buchwald J. S., 'Proprioceptive reflexes and posture', *American Journal of Physical Medicine,* 1967 vol. 46, pp. 104-113.
9. *Structure and Function of the Nervous System,* p. 77.
10. ibid., pp. 237, 238.
11. *Structure of the Human Body,* pp. 300, 301.
12. *Function of the Human Body,* p. 261; *Kinesiology,* p. 168.
13. *Structure and Function of the Nervous System,* p. 166.
14. *Structure of the Human Body,* p. 160.
15. *Structure and Function of the Nervous System,* pp. 161, 162; *Kinesiology,* pp. 169, 170.
16. *Understanding the Scientific Bases of Human Movement,* p. 201.
17. *Primary Anatomy,* pp. 315, 316, 317; *Structure and Function of Nervous System,* chap. 17; *Structure of the Human Body,* pp. 281-284. Messages also pass to the lower brain and brain stem where centres control the autonomic system, consisting of the sympathetic and parasympathetic systems of nerves. These nerves arise from the brain stem and spinal cord and travel in the mixed nerves (page 19). The two systems work as a plus and minus balance of the whole body controlling glands, organs, and the involuntary muscle interlining blood vessels, etc., which are not controlled by the consciousness. In the fear reflex the sympathetic nervous system produces changes in glands and blood vessels, etc., to help the activity of fighting or running.

CHAPTER 3

1. Knott M. and Voss D., *Proprioceptive Neuromuscular Facilitation,* Hoeber-Harper, 1963, pp. 6-9.
2. *Primary Anatomy,* pp. 115-116.
3. Russell R., *Explaining the Brain,* Oxford University Press, 1975, Preface p. 1.
4. *Structure and Function of the Nervous System,* pp. 6-8, 200, 201.
5. *Explaining the Brain,* pp. 1-6.
6. *Understanding the Scientific Bases of Human Movement,* pp. 224, 225.
7. *Explaining the Brain,* pp. 10-13, 16.
8. *Structure and Function of the Nervous System,* p. 81.
9. ibid., pp. 200, 201.
10. Anderson T., *Human Kinetics and Analysing Body Movements,* Heinemann, 1951, pp. 113-118.
11. *Function of the Human Body,* pp. 268, 269.
12. Benson H., *The Relaxation Response,* Collins, 1976, pp. 68, 69.
13. Gardener D., *Principles of Exercise Therapy,* Bell, 3rd edition 1973, pp. 144, 145.
14. *Understanding the Scientific Bases of Human Movement,* pp. 151, 152.
15. *Structure and Function of the Nervous System,* p. 47.
16. *Kinesiology,* p. 171; Basmajian J., *Muscles Alive,* Williams and Watkins, 2nd edition 1967, pp. 72-74.
17. *The Relaxation Response,* pp. 65-67.
18. *Muscles Alive,* pp. 86-88, 92, 342; *Kinesiology,* pp. 42-45, 175, 176; *Understanding the Scientific Bases of Human Movement,* p. 30.
19. ibid., p. 200.

CHAPTER 4

1. *Structure and Function of the Nervous System,* pp. 237, 238.
2. *Principles of Exercise Therapy,* p. 63.
3. *Structure and Function of the Nervous System,* pp. 237, 238.
4. Ibid.
5. *Function of the Human Body,* p. 196.
6. *Structure and Function of the Nervous System,* p. 99.
7. *The Principles of Exercise Therapy,* p. 147.
8. *Structure and Function of the Nervous System,* pp. 241, 242.

CHAPTER 5

1. *Understanding the Scientific Bases of Human Movement,* p. 219.
2. *Structure and Function of the Nervous System,* pp. 241, 242.
3. Rodahl K., *Be Fit for Life,* Allen and Unwin, 1968, pp. 109-115.
4. ibid., p. 106.
5. Mitchell J. C., 'Dermatological Aspects of Displacement Activity', *Canadian Medical Association Journal,* vol. 98 1968, p. 962-964.
6. Alexander F. M. and Maisel E., *The Alexander Technique,* Thames and Hudson, 1975, introduction part 1, chap. 5.

CHAPTER 6

1. *Be Fit for Life*, pp. 106, 107.
2. *The Alexander Technique,* appendix III. *Human Kinetics and Analysing Body Movement,* p. 97.
3. Gaskell D. and Webber B., *The Brompton Hospital Guide to Chest Physiotherapy,* Blackwell Scientific Publications, 2nd edition 1975, pp. 1-6; *The Human Body,* pp. 32-43.
4. *Principles of Anatomy and Physiology for Training Instructors in the R.A.F.,* H.M. Stationery Office, 3rd edition 1962, p. 136.
5. *Primary Anatomy,* pp. 215, 216.
6. ibid., pp. 230, 233, 234.
7. ibid., p. 216.
8. *Kinesiology,* p. 217; *Structure of the Human Body,* pp. 198, 200.
9. *Primary Anatomy,* pp. 46-48.
10. *Brompton Hospital Guide to Chest Physiotherapy,* pp. 22-26, 29.
11. Halberg F., 'The 24 Hour Scale' *Perspectives in Biology and Medicine,* 1960, p. 491.
12. *Pregnancy,* pp. 106, 107, 151.
13. ibid., pp. 103, 105

CHAPTER 7

1. *The Relaxation Response.*
2. ibid., Chap. 7.
3. *Understanding the Scientific Bases of Human Movement,* pp. 35-48.
4. *Be Fit for Life,* Chap. 10.

FURTHER READING

Backhouse K. M., 'Functional Anatomy of the Hand', *Physiotherapy Magazine,* 1968 April.

Buzan A., *Use Your Head,* BBC Publications, 1976.

Carruthers Malcolm, *The Western Way of Death,* Davis-Poynter, 1974.

Cratty Bryant J., *Teaching Motor Skills,* Prentice Hall Inc., 1973.

Fink D. H., *Release from Nervous Tension,* Allen and Unwin, 1954.

Francis Dick, *For Kicks,* (a perfect exposition of the fear reflex) Michael Joseph, 1965.

Garmany G., *Muscle Relaxation,* Actinic Press, 1952.

Harding Geoffrey, *Guide to Stress,* Guild church of St Mary Woolnoth, London E.C.3., 1975.

Israel Martin, *The Power of the Spirit in Everyday Living,* Churches' Fellowship for Psychical and Spiritual Studies, 1971.

Mackean D. and Jones B., *Introduction to Human and Social Biology,* John Murray, 1975.

Melzack Ronald, *The Puzzle of Pain,* Penguin, 1973.

Montagu Ashley, *Touching,* Perennial Library Columbia University Press, 1971.

Russell-Brain W., *Mind, Perception, and Science,* Blackwell, 1951.

Wright Beric H., *Executive Ease and Dis-ease,* Gower Press, 1975.

INDEX

Now that you are relaxed, here's the book to get you moving again, in the right way.

Simple Movement

THE WHY AND HOW OF EXERCISE

Laura Mitchell and Barbara Dale

Exercise is a vital ingredient of life. If this is the first time you have faced up to your need for it *Simple Movement* will give you a firm grounding in the theory before leading you through a sequence of carefully graded exercises.

If you have already tried yoga, modern dance, gymnastics or advanced keep-fit and found them difficult, *Simple Movement* will help to get you off the mark again. The emphasis throughout is on a thorough, professional approach, making a start from first principles and tackling the simple but vital routines.

The book begins with your most fundamental movements: the flow of messages through your brain and nerves, the circulation of blood, the rhythm of breathing, the movement of muscles and bones beneath the skin, the continual mass of small adjustments that keep your standing or sitting posture correct. The basic physical laws of gravity, leverage and atmospheric pressure that dictate to the body are explained. Only once the reasons that lie behind—the Why of exercise—have been discussed, does the book open out into the How, its own sequence of thirty exercises. Nearly all these simple movements are performed in a sitting or lying position. While not spectacular, they are safe and, if done conscientiously, make a satisfying course in themselves as well as providing a firm foundation for any more complex and demanding activity that you might go on to.

The final chapters fit movement into the pattern of every-day life and describe exercises to be done in the bath, shower or bed, office, kitchen or garden, as well as offering hints for the old and disabled.

224 pages

20 line drawings and diagrams

46 photographs

hardback and paperback